FABRIC SAVVY

The Essential Guide for Every Sewer

Sandra Betzina

The Taunton Press

PUBLISHER
JIM CHILDS

ACQUISITIONS EDITOR
JOLYNN GOWER

EDITORIAL ASSISTANT
SARAH COE

EDITOR
CAROLYN MANDARANO

INDEXER
LYNDA STANNARD

DESIGNER
MARY TERRIZZI

LAYOUT ARTIST
ROSALIE VACCARO

PHOTOGRAPHER
JACK DEUTSCH

ILLUSTRATOR
ROBERT LA POINTE

The Taunton Press
Inspiration for hands-on living™

Text © 2002 by Sandra Betzina
Photographs © 2002 by The Taunton Press, Inc.
Illustrations © 2002 by The Taunton Press, Inc.

Fabric Savvy was originally published in hardcover in 1999 by The Taunton Press, Inc.

Distributed by Publishers Group West

The Taunton Press, Inc., 63 South Main Street, PO Box 5506, Newtown, CT 06470-5506
e-mail: tp@taunton.com

Library of Congress Cataloging-in-Publication Data

Betzina, Sandra.
        Fabric savvy : essential advice for every sewer / Sandra Betzina.
                p.   cm.
        Includes index.
        ISBN 1-56158-573-4
        1. Textile fabrics. 2. Dressmaking materials. I. Title.
TT557.B48   1999   98-44107
646'.11—dc21   CIP

Printed in the United States of America
10 9 8 7 6 5 4 3 2 1

To my husband Dan, whose excitement and enthusiasm affect every aspect of our lives.

Acknowledgments

The idea for this book came from the popularity of my class entitled "Fashion and Fabric of the '90s." The initial research began by reading everything I could get my hands on about fabric. The next step took place at the sewing machine, experimenting and critiquing results. After compiling my finds, I sent my research to three individuals who have commanded my respect over a long period of time: Joann Banko, Carlene Jones, and Kenneth King. I encouraged them to disagree with me or add from their experience. Each suggestion was tested. Once again the results were compiled. To the best of my knowledge, this is the most practical, up-to-date, complete information on the subject of fabric.

While most of the garments in this book are my creations, a few individuals did such an outstanding job on their garments that I felt they must be included for inspiration. Special thanks to Karie Aineb for the velveteen jumper, Deborah Darlington for the fur-trimmed water- and wind-resistant parka, Sarah Dennis and Toby Haberman for the beaded dresses, Susan Huxley for the vinyl pants, Mary Anne Martines for the silk shantung child's dress, Paula O'Connell for the his-and-hers ski suits, Lizanne and Rick Reitmeiser for the waterproof breathable anorak and wetsuit, Helen Snell for the long velveteen coat, Mary Stori for the silk noil dress, Shanlee Tyler for the windbloc coat, and Pat Williams for the sequin strapless dress.

Special thanks as well as to those who have shared their knowledge in writing: Naomi Baker, Harriett Baskett, Karen Bennett, Fred Bloebaum, Judith Brandau, Grad Callaway, Bobbie Carr, Ronda Chaney, Clotilde, Ron Collins, Leah Crain, Mary Ann Crawford, Carol Cruise, Kerdene De Priest, Sally Erickson, Linda Faiola, Kathleen Fasanella, Shermane Fouché, Mona Freeman, Henry Galler, Debbie Garbers, Ellen Gienger, Giselle Gilson, Arlene Haidys, Elke Haines, Gale Hazen, Cheryl Holliday, Laura Hotchkins Brown, Karen Howland, Jane Jasper, Collen Jones, Marsha Jorgensen, Barbara Kelly, Susan Khalje, Margaret Komives, Elea Scott Landis, Jeanne Leavit, Mary Ellen McKee, Heather Millette, Karen Morris, Nancy Nehring, Janet O'Brien, Pamela Peltier, Marlie Popple, Elizabeth Rhodes, Rita Sue Ronse, Helen Rose, Donna Salyers, Jan Saunders, Claire Schaeffer, Anne Marie Soto, Ferne Taylor, Marcy Tilton, and Cynthia Tyndall.

Contents

Introduction

Walking into a fabric store can be overwhelming. Shelves are lined with gorgeous new fabrics and an array of notions you may never have tried. Many students comment to me about the beautiful and exciting new fabrics they find and ask me what needle, presser foot, stitch length, and interfacing they need to use. Few have the courage to experiment themselves.

Fabric Savvy takes all of the guesswork out of working with new fabrics and old favorites. It tips you off to successful styles, whether or not preshrinking is necessary, what interfacing to use, and which needle, presser foot, stitch length, layout, seam finishes, closures, hem, and pressing techniques will yield the most professional results on that particular fabric. *Fabric Savvy* also gives you any special sewing and fitting tips you might need. The format makes the information easy to find so that you can look up just what you need when you need it. For those who really like to sew, this book will be indispensable.

African Mudcloth

PRESHRINK
Overlock crossgrain ends. Machine-wash in warm water and machine-dry at normal temperature to remove mud residue, which makes it somewhat stiff.

LAYOUT
Without nap, single layer to position pattern pieces to make the best of motifs.

MARKING
Clo-Chalk.

CUTTING
Although it is okay to cut fabric double thickness, you may save fabric by cutting single thickness, since fabric is sold by the piece rather than by the yard.

INTERFACING
French Fuse or Fuse-Knit.

THREAD
Good-quality polyester or cotton.

NEEDLE
80/12 H.

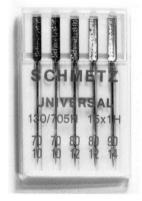

STITCH LENGTH
2.5 mm.

PRESSER FOOT
Standard.

SEAM FINISH
Flat fell or bind with double-fold bias. (See #9 on p. 175, #20 on p. 177.)

PRESSING
Steam iron on cotton setting.

TOPSTITCHING
Doesn't show up.

CLOSURES
For buttonholes use 70/10 HJ needle and water-soluble stabilizer between presser foot and feed dogs.

HEM
Hand-hem. (See #4 on p. 187.)

African mudcloth

FABRIC FACT
African mudcloth is a rather firm ethnic fabric that is woven in 6-in.-wide strips and joined by hand to form fabric width.

SUITABLE FOR
Vests, structured tops, jackets. Choose garment styles with minimum seaming to avoid breaking up fabric design. Avoid princess styling.

SEWING TIPS
Easy to sew.

Tip: Clo-Chalk is a disappearing chalk that leaves no residue.

Alpaca

PRESHRINK

Hold steam iron ½ in. above fabric or preshrink at the dry cleaner.

LAYOUT

Right side is obvious on a woven. Press foldline to see if crease is permanent, and if so, cut around it. With nap, double thickness. Hairs go down. To determine right side on single knits, stretch the fabric. It will roll to right side.

MARKING

Tailor tacks or tailor's chalk.

CUTTING

Rotary cutter or sharp scissors, pattern weights.

INTERFACING

No fusible; sew-in only. If you are making a tailored jacket, underline entire jacket with cotton batiste or voile. Armo Weft can then be fused to underlining before it is attached to the fashion fabric.

THREAD

Silk machine twist is preferred. Good-quality polyester or cotton is suitable.

NEEDLE

80/12 H on wovens, 75/11 HS on knits.

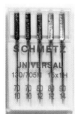 

STITCH LENGTH

Wovens—2.5 mm straight stitch; knits—tiny zigzag (0.5 mm width, 2.0 mm length).

PRESSER FOOT

Wovens—standard; knits—walking.

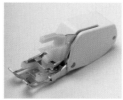

SEAM FINISH

Wovens—no seam finish if lined, otherwise pink or serge each piece separately with 3-thread overlock. Knits—sew first with tiny zigzag, then serge together. (See #2 and #3 on p. 174, #21 on p. 177.)

PRESSING

Steam iron on wool setting, using press-and-lift motion. Always use a self-fabric press cloth on right side.

TOPSTITCHING

Not recommended. Instead, hand-pick with sulky rayon or buttonhole twist on wovens ½ in. from finished edge with stitches ½ in. apart. (See #1 on p. 180.)

CLOSURES

Wovens—corded machine, hand, or bound buttonholes. (See #2 and #5 on p. 182, #8 on p. 183.) Knit cardigans—press ¼ in. toward wrong side of front. Cover with grosgrain ribbon. Sew long sides of grosgrain with ribbon against presser foot and knit against feed dogs, then make machine buttonholes with 70/10 HJ needle and extra-fine thread. (See #7 on p. 183.)

HEM

Wovens—hand-hem. (See #4 on p. 187.) Knits—serge bottom of knit with differential feed or with finger pushing into the back of presser foot to keep the knit from stretching. Sew two rows of double-needle topstitching with woolly nylon thread hand-wrapped on bobbin and a double-needle ZWI stretch. Topstitch using a walking foot to keep the knit from stretching. Loosen top tension until double row of stitches lies flat. (See #1 on p. 187.)

Alpaca

FABRIC FACT
Alpaca is a close relative to cashmere in its softness and luxury. It is also very warm to wear without being bulky, so if you get hot easily, this fabric is not for you.

SUITABLE FOR
Woven alpaca makes a beautiful jacket or coat. Knitted alpaca makes a nice sweater top, cardigan, clingy dress, or gored skirt. Since alpaca is available in both knits and wovens and is fairly costly, I suggest pretesting the pattern. Ripped stitches weaken the fabric.

SEWING TIPS
Lift fabric every 6 in. and smooth out. Stabilize neckline and shoulders with twill tape or ¼-in.-wide selvage strips.

Tip: If you are having difficulty sliding a jacket into position under the buttonhole foot, it will not feed properly for a flawless buttonhole. Consider other alternatives such as button loops or snaps or facing the opening in a lighter weight fabric like wool jersey.

Arctic Fleece

PRESHRINK

No preshrinking necessary. After construction, machine-wash alone or with other fleece garments in cool water, machine-dry on low setting. Remove immediately. Reduce abrasion by turning the garment inside out. Do not dry-clean.

LAYOUT

"With nap" layout, double-layer cutting okay. To determine right side of fabric, pull on crossgrain; fabric curls to wrong side. Be consistent with which side of the fabric you use, as the pile height may differ. Use pattern weights.

MARKING

Chalk, fabric markers, smooth tracing wheel. Identify wrong side with tape or chalk.

CUTTING

Scissors or large rotary cutter. Cut with a ¼-in. seam allowance.

INTERFACING

None, except for zippers. Use nonfusible interfacing in the seam allowance since the pressing required to fuse a fusible will crush the nap.

THREAD

Good-quality polyester.

NEEDLE

70/10 H, 80/12 H, 75/11 HS, or 90/14 HS for thicker varieties. Arctic fleece is not needle choosy. 70/10 HM, 80/12 HM on windbloc.

STITCH LENGTH

3.0 mm straight stitch. Use stretch stitch in crotch seams.

PRESSER FOOT

Satin stitch foot (also known as appliqué foot) eliminates wavy, stretched seams where regular construction is used.

SEAM FINISH

For a durable, attractive finish, finger-press seam open and topstitch with a double-needle ZWI stretch 4.0 mm from the right side. Trim seam allowances close to stitching. Or construct with 4-thread overlock and lengthen stitch slightly.

Use differential feed if you have it. If not, sew with finger behind presser foot as with easing. (See #5 on p. 174, #13 on p. 176.) For windbloc, sew seams with 4-thread overlock. Do not topstitch since it makes the garment less waterproof. Seam sealant cannot be applied to seams.

PRESSING

No pressing.

TOPSTITCHING

¼ in. from edge. Lengthen stitch to 4.0 mm or longer. (See #10 on p. 181.) No topstitching on windbloc.

CLOSURES

YKK plastic zippers. Snaps must be reinforced with sew-in interfacing between layers to prevent them from pulling out of the fabric. (See #11 on p. 184, #19 on p. 186.) Machine buttonholes stretch out.

HEM

Since fleece does not ravel, edges can be left without a finish, pinked, topstitched with double needle, overlocked with decorative thread on needles and woolly nylon on loopers, bound with faux leather or a knit cut on the crossgrain, or blanket stitched on the serger or by hand. Ribbing is also popular. (See #32 on p. 192.)

Arctic fleece

FABRIC FACT
Synthetic fleece is a knit fabric that stretches on the crossgrain. It sheds water, holds body heat, but allows perspiration to escape. Polar Fleece by Malden Mills is the best since it pills and stretches the least. In generic brand fleece, look for the "anti-pill" factor. Fleece is comfortable and warm and survives years of abuse. Polartec Windbloc by Malden Mills is a soft fleece fabric that is windproof, water-proof, and breathable. A water-repellent finish sheds water and snow. This fabric has the same insulation as wool with half its weight.

SUITABLE FOR
Arctic fleece is great for sweatshirts, pull-on pants, short cropped jackets, vests. Windbloc is great for jackets, ski wear, and rain suits.

SEWING TIPS
If you notice any seam stretching as you sew, place finger behind presser foot as with easing. Stabilize crotch and shoul-der seams with ¼-in.-wide clear elastic.

Tip: On high-loft fabrics such as polyfleece, fake fur, and mohair, pattern weights are far more effective than pins in securing the pattern to the fabric.

Beaded

PRESHRINK
Not necessary.

LAYOUT
Single layer; check to see if the beaded design has a direction. If so, cut as "with nap" layout. Be careful when you take off the tape the store puts on the crossgrain. A sudden rip of the tape will start a run in the beads lengthwise. Place beaded fabric, with bead side up, against color-contrasted surface so that you can see the design. Consider design placement when placing the pattern pieces.

MARKING
Tailor tacks.

CUTTING
Pattern weights are preferred since pins tear the pattern tissue. Don't use your best scissors as beads will mar the blades.

INTERFACING
Tulle or silk organza.

THREAD
Good-quality cotton or polyester.

NEEDLE
90/14 HJ. Have plenty on hand since beads break and dull needles quickly.

STITCH LENGTH
2.0 mm straight stitch.

PRESSER FOOT
Since beads are removed from seams and darts, sew seams with zipper foot to prevent foot from riding over the beads. Sew seams with the edge of the foot against the ridge of the beads.

SEAM FINISH
If you are not lining, finish each side of seam allowance with Seams Great or bias lining

strips in a Hong Kong finish. (See #16 and #19 on p. 176.) Eliminate facings. Finish neck and armholes with bias silk charmeuse, or use a separate lining attached at neck and armholes only. Bias binder attachment works well here. Examine seams for bald spots. Hand-sew beads in any bald spots.

PRESSING
With low-temperature iron, press seams open over towel.

TOPSTITCHING
Never. Hand-picking close to edge can help flatten seam. (See #1 on p. 180.)

CLOSURES
Consider buttonhole alternatives like button loops or faced buttonhole openings. Zipper must be hand-picked. (See #5 on p. 180, #6 and #9 on p. 183.)

HEM
Hong Kong finish the raw edge of the beaded fabric with bias lining strips. Turn up hem. Whipstitch drapery weights to the hem fold. Hand-hem garment and lining separately. (See #13 on p. 189.)

Beaded

FABRIC FACT
Since this fabric is expensive, think of it as only part of a garment. It can be used just for details, such as a collar and pocket flaps.

SUITABLE FOR
Evening wear, bodices, and jackets. Choose a pattern with as few seams and darts as possible. Consider eliminating straight side seams and cutting all in one piece. Pretest the pattern.

SEWING TIPS
Underline with silk tulle, which can be dyed to match the beaded fabric. After cutting beaded fabric, cut identical pieces in tulle and lining. Use an upholstery hammer or pliers to smash beads in the seam allowances. This makes them easier to remove and leaves threads intact. Use safety goggles or sunglasses to protect eyes. Pull beads out of all seam allowances. (See #35 on p. 179.) Do not brush beads away with hands since many beads are glass, and crushed beads can have sharp edges. Using a zipper foot, staystitch around all edges of the beaded fabric at ⅝ in. Run a bead of clear glue right next to staystitch line on the seam allowance. With tulle sandwiched between the beaded fabric and the lining, hand-baste together. Stabilize shoulder seams with narrow lining selvage or stay-tape. Line entire garment with silk organza or charmeuse, depending on the crispness you want.

Boiled Wool

PRESHRINK
Not necessary.

LAYOUT
"Without nap" layout, single thickness, pattern weights.

MARKING
Clo-Chalk or tailor tacks.

CUTTING
Rotary cutter or scissors.

INTERFACING
None—fabric has enough body without it.

THREAD
Good-quality cotton, polyester, or silk.

NEEDLE
90/14 H.

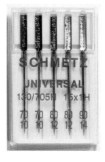

STITCH LENGTH
3.0 mm.

PRESSER FOOT
Teflon or standard.

SEAM FINISH
Sew seams. Clip curves. Press seam open. Topstitch on each side of seam from right side using the wide double-needle ZWI 6.0 mm, or topstitch each side separately ⅛ in. to ¼ in. from seam. Trim seam allowances close to topstitching. (See #13 on p. 176.)

PRESSING
Steam iron on wool setting. Use press cloth when pressing on the right side.

TOPSTITCHING
On both sides of seams ⅛ in. to ¼ in. from seam.

CLOSURES
Corded buttonholes through a single layer. (See #5 on p. 182.) Use stabilizer between the fabric and the feed dogs. Since a corded buttonhole through a single layer is fragile, consider a faced buttonhole (see #6 on p. 183) or button loops (see #9 on p. 183) on a garment that will be buttoned frequently. Back buttons on the wrong side of the fabric with small buttons to prevent buttons from pulling away from the fabric.

HEM
Eliminate hem allowance. Staystitch finished edge at ¼ in. to prevent stretching. There are several options for finishing edges: 1) fold-over knitted braid sewn on by hand (see #11 on p. 188); 2) strips of crossgrain-cut wool jersey or faux leather; 3) blanket stitch by hand using yarn; or 4) decorative serger stitch using shiny rayon thread.

Boiled wool

FABRIC FACT

Boiled wool is a felted knitted wool that has the flexibility of a knit while providing great warmth. Boiled wool cardigans are sold by Jaeger. You can create your own version of boiled wool by machine washing a loosely knitted wool in hot water and Ivory Soap flakes. Agitate in washing machine for 30 minutes. Machine-dry in hot dryer. Fabric will shrink approximately 40% to 50% in both directions.

SUITABLE FOR

Fitted styles with princess seam in lieu of darts, or boxy styles. Think of a garment in boiled wool like a sweater. To reduce bulk, eliminate hem, facings, and linings.

SEWING TIPS

Stabilize neck, shoulders, and top edge of pockets with stay-tape. Single-layer patch pockets are the least bulky. Finish top of pocket with trim. Machine-sew pocket to garment with machine blanket stitch. Boiled wool is a good candidate for machine or hand-embroidery. Pin tucking with the double needle creates an attractive raised design detail.

Tip: Silk and rayon threads give a lustrous sheen.

Camel Hair

PRESHRINK
Hold steam iron ½ in. above fabric or preshrink at the dry cleaner.

LAYOUT
Right side is obvious on a woven. Press foldline to see if crease is permanent; if so, cut around. Hairs go down. With nap, double thickness.

MARKING
Tailor tacks or tailor's chalk.

CUTTING
Rotary cutter or sharp scissors, pattern weights.

INTERFACING
No fusible; sew-in only. If you are making a tailored jacket, underline entire jacket with cotton batiste or voile. Armo Weft can then be fused to underlining before it is attached to the fashion fabric.

THREAD
Silk machine twist is preferred. Good-quality polyester or cotton is suitable.

NEEDLE
80/12 H.

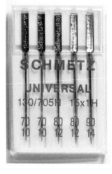

STITCH LENGTH
2.5 mm straight stitch.

PRESSER FOOT
Standard.

SEAM FINISH
No seam finish if lined; otherwise pink or serge each piece separately with 3-thread overlock. (See #2 and #3 on p. 174.)

PRESSING
Steam iron on wool setting, using press-and-lift motion. Always use a self-fabric press cloth on the right side.

TOPSTITCHING
Not recommended. Instead, hand-pick with sulky rayon or buttonhole twist ½ in. from the finished edge with stitches ½ in. apart. (See #1 on p. 180.)

CLOSURES
Corded machine, hand, or bound buttonholes. (See #2 and #5 on p. 182, #8 on p. 183.)

HEM
Hand-hem. (See #4 on p. 187.)

Camel hair

FABRIC FACT

Camel hair is a close relative to cashmere in its softness and luxury. It is also very warm to wear without being bulky, so if you get hot easily, this fabric is not for you.

SUITABLE FOR

Woven camel hair makes a beautiful jacket or coat. Since camel hair is fairly costly, I would suggest pretesting the pattern. Ripped stitches weaken the fabric.

SEWING TIPS

Lift fabric every 6 in. and smooth out. Stabilize neckline and shoulders with twill tape or ¼-in.-wide selvage.

Tip: Before pressing outer edge of lapels, hand-baste from the top side, favoring the way you want the garment to look. Silk thread has elasticity and prevents thread imprint during pressing. Cover top side with press cloth, spray for moisture, press and pound flat with tailor's clapper.

Cashmere

PRESHRINK

Hold steam iron ½ in. above fabric or preshrink at dry cleaner.

LAYOUT

Right side is obvious on a woven. To determine right side on a knit, stretch knit; fabric will roll to the right side. Press foldline flat to see if crease is permanent; if so, cut around it. Use "with nap" layout, double thickness.

MARKING

Tailor tacks, tailor's chalk, fabric markers.

CUTTING

Rotary cutter or sharp scissors, pattern weights.

INTERFACING

Textured Weft or Armo Weft. If you are making a jacket, consider underlining the entire jacket with cotton batiste or voile. Interfacing can then be fused to underlining. The advantages to this are that the character of the fabric is maintained by not fusing directly onto the fabric and that all hand stitches can be attached to the underlining.

THREAD

Silk machine twist is preferred. Good-quality polyester or cotton is suitable.

NEEDLE

80/12 H on wovens, 75/11 HS on knits.

STITCH LENGTH

Wovens—2.5 mm straight stitch; knits— tiny zigzag (0.5 mm width, 2.0 mm length).

PRESSER FOOT

Wovens—standard; knits—walking.

SEAM FINISH

Wovens—no seam finish if lined; otherwise pink or serge each piece separately with 3-thread overlock. (See #2 and #3 on p. 174.) Knits— sew first with tiny zigzag, then serge together. (See #21 on p. 177.)

PRESSING

Steam iron on wool setting. Use press-and-lift motion. Always use a self-fabric press cloth on the right side.

TOPSTITCHING

Not recommended. Instead, hand-pick with sulky rayon or buttonhole twist on wovens, ⅜ in. from the finished edge with stitches ⅜ in. apart. (See #1 on p. 180.)

CLOSURES

Wovens—corded machine, hand, or bound buttonholes. (See #2 and #5 on p. 182, #8 on p. 183.) Knit cardigans—press ¼ in. toward wrong side of front. Cover with grosgrain ribbon. Sew long sides of grosgrain with it on top and knit against feed dogs. Make machine buttonholes with 70/10 HJ needle and extra-fine thread. (See #7 on p. 183.)

HEM

Wovens—hand-hem. (See #4 on p. 187.) Knits—serge bottom of knit using differential feed or pushing behind presser foot with finger to keep from stretching. Sew two rows of double-needle topstitching with woolly nylon thread hand-wrapped on bobbin and double-needle ZWI stretch. Topstitch using a walking foot to keep knit from stretching. Loosen top tension until double row of stitches lies flat. Or use cover hem topstitch or flatlock hem stitch. (See #1, #2, and #5 on p. 187.)

Cashmere

FABRIC FACT
Cashmere is the #1 luxury fabric in softness and warmth without bulk.

SUITABLE FOR
Woven cashmere makes a beautiful jacket or coat. Knitted cashmere makes a nice sweater top, cardigan, clingy dress, gored skirt, or luxurious bathrobe. Since cashmere is available in both knits and wovens and is fairly costly, I suggest pretesting the pattern. Ripped stitches weaken the fabric.

Tip: Prevent a raised welt when using the double needle for topstitching by loosening top tension slightly.

SEWING TIPS
Lift fabric every 6 in. and smooth out. Stabilize neckline and shoulders with twill tape or selvage strips.

Chenille

PRESHRINK

Turn wrong side out. Hand-wash or machine-wash on gentle cycle with warm water. Dry flat.

LAYOUT

"With nap" layout, double thickness. Use pattern weights.

MARKING

Tailor tacks seem to be the only thing that will show up.

CUTTING

Scissors or rotary cutter.

INTERFACING

Fuse-Knit or French Fuse.

THREAD

Good-quality cotton or polyester.

NEEDLE

80/12 H.

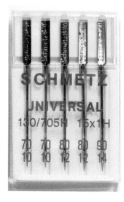

STITCH LENGTH

2.0 mm.

PRESSER FOOT

Walking or Teflon.

SEAM FINISH

Sew seam with straight stitch. Press open. Serge each side of seam separately if not already serged, or bind each side of seam with Seams Great. (See #3 on p. 174, #19 on p. 176.)

PRESSING

Cover pressing surface with fluffy towel. Place right side of chenille against towel. Press on cotton setting with steam. No pressing on right side of the nap—it flattens it.

TOPSTITCHING

Not recommended.

CLOSURES

Corded buttonhole, buttonhole in a seam, faced buttonhole, bound buttonhole in contrasting fabric. (See #5 on p. 182, #6, #8, and #10 on p. 183.)

HEM

Serge raw edge or finish with Seams Great. Hand-hem. (See #4 on p. 187, #14 on p. 189.)

Chenille

FABRIC FACT

This soft-to-the-touch fabric wears better and does not stretch out of shape if it is fully interfaced with Fuse-Knit. If you prefer the soft drapiness, choose a style where slight stretching is acceptable.

SUITABLE FOR

Vest or jacket (must be fully interfaced); big shirt, loose top, or bathrobe (use as is).

SEWING TIPS

Overlock all pieces separately right after fusing or cutting if using as is. Pushing fabric toward the presser foot rather than letting the feeding move the fabric along prevents the fabric from stretching as you sew.

Tip: Most sergers have needles that are interchangeable with conventional sewing machines. Changing serger needles to match fabric is especially important on microfibers and silks.

China Silk

PRESHRINK
Hand-wash in shampoo, then air-dry. Press while damp.

LAYOUT
"Without nap" layout, double thickness.

MARKING
Tracing paper, fabric markers, Clo-Chalk.

CUTTING
Rotary cutter or sharp scissors.

INTERFACING
None.

THREAD
Fine machine embroidery in good-quality cotton, polyester, or silk.

NEEDLE
65/9 H, 70/10 H.

STITCH LENGTH
2.0 mm.

PRESSER FOOT
Standard. Switch needle to far left position to get support on all three sides. Or use single-needle presser foot and small-hole throat plate.

SEAM FINISH
Pinked or none if lining is fully enclosed.

PRESSING
Silk setting, dry iron. Press seams as sewn before pressing open.

TOPSTITCHING
None.

CLOSURES
None.

HEM
Double roll ½-in. hem, then machine-stitch. (See #10 on p. 188.)

China silk

FABRIC FACT
China silk is a very lightweight plain weave silk. It is used for lining because it breathes.

SUITABLE FOR
Linings only; too thin for garments.

SEWING TIPS
Pull fabric taut from front and back as you sew.

Tip: Wash-away fabric markers may "bleed" into fabric. These are great products, but keep these guidelines in mind:

• **Always test first to see if the marks are easily removed.**

• **Remove marks with clear cool water first, then wash in detergent.**

• **Do not press over ink, as the heat from the iron may set the marks permanently.**

• **"Green" liquid detergents such as Palmolive may also set the ink permanently.**

Corduroy

PRESHRINK

Turn fabric right side in and stitch ends together. Machine-wash in warm water and dry on delicate cycle. If you plan to dry-clean finished garment, hold steam iron ½ in. above surface. Care: Turn inside out, machine-wash, and dry on delicate cycle. Dry cleaning keeps the garment new looking longer. Restore flattened pile by tumbling corduroy, wrong side out, with damp towel for 10 minutes. Avoid lint transfer by putting a dark-colored towel in with dark-colored corduroy, light-colored towel with light-colored corduroy. Take out of dryer and immediately hang up.

LAYOUT

"With nap" layout, double thickness. Pile wears better if pieces are cut with nap going down. For richer color, cut with nap going up. Place fabric wrong sides together for cutting accuracy.

MARKING

Clo-Chalk, fabric markers, pencils, tailor tacks.

CUTTING

Rotary cutter or scissors. Use smooth cotton for facings to eliminate bulk.

INTERFACING

Sew-in such as Pellon Pel-Aire.

THREAD

Good-quality cotton or polyester.

NEEDLE

80/12 HJ or 80/12 H.

STITCH LENGTH

2.5 mm straight stitch.

PRESSER FOOT

Walking or roller foot. Loosen top tension slightly.

SEAM FINISH

Serge piece separately or enclose in flat-fell seams. (See #3 on p. 174, #9 on p. 175.)

PRESSING

Cover pressing surface with fluffy towel, self-fabric, velvet board, or needle board. Iron on cotton setting with steam. Press with point of iron in seam allowance. Avoid pressing on right side of fabric.

TOPSTITCHING

Not recommended.

CLOSURES

For buttonholes, use 70/10 HJ and fine machine embroidery thread to reduce bulk. Lengthen and widen stitch slightly. Before opening buttonholes, apply Fray Stop to buttonhole. Let dry, then cut open. This controls shredding of corduroy around buttonhole. (See #4 on p. 182.) Place hanging loops inside waistband to avoid crushing pile with pinchers on hangers.

HEM

Hand-hem. (See #4 on p. 187.)

Corduroy

FABRIC FACT
Corduroy is derived from the French *cordon du roi,* which means cord of kings.

SUITABLE FOR
Vests, straight skirts, tailored shirts, structured jackets, jumpers, tailored pants, and children's clothes. Corduroy is especially flattering in dark colors on adults.

SEWING TIPS
Sew in direction of pile.

Tip: If you are heavy, avoid wide-wale corduroy since it adds bulk.

Cotton Batiste

PRESHRINK
Hand-wash in Ivory flakes. Drip-dry.

LAYOUT
Check for permanent crease at foldline. Re-fold to avoid. "Without nap" layout, double thickness.

MARKING
Fabric markers or pencils.

CUTTING
Rotary cutter or scissors.

INTERFACING
Self-fabric.

THREAD
Fine cotton machine embroidery.

NEEDLE
60/8 H or 70/10 HM.

STITCH LENGTH
2.0 mm.

PRESSER FOOT
Use single-hole presser foot and small-hole throat plate or switch needle to the far left position for support on three sides. Loosen top tension and bottom tension one-eighth to one-quarter of a turn.

SEAM FINISH
French seams or 3-thread overlock with super-fine serger thread such as Janome over-lock polyester thread #80. (See #4 on p. 174, #10 on p. 175.)

PRESSING
Cotton setting with steam. Use spray starch to crispen.

TOPSTITCHING
Close to finished edge. Use edge foot or edge-joining foot for accuracy.

CLOSURES
For buttonholes, use 60/8 H new needle and fine cotton machine embroidery thread to reduce bulk. (See #1 on p. 182.)

HEM
Hand-stitch, machine decorative, or lace. (See #12 on p. 188, #13 on p. 189.)

Cotton batiste

FABRIC FACT
Cotton batiste is often used as underlining or as backing for soft cotton quilts.

SUITABLE FOR
100% Swiss cotton batiste is preferred for heirloom sewing because the lace on the polyester blends does not lie as flat. When used as underlining, polyester blends are not quite as good because they do not breathe.

SEWING TIPS
Staystitching is very important.

Tip: **WISTFUL** by Springmaid, a cotton/polyester-blend batiste, makes an excellent underlining because it doesn't collapse in wearing. **WISTFUL** is a good substitute for 100% cotton batiste, which is expensive.

Cotton Damask

PRESHRINK

Machine-wash in warm water and machine-dry on regular temperature.

LAYOUT

"Without nap" layout, double thickness.

MARKING

Clo-Chalk, fabric marking pens, tracing paper.

CUTTING

Rotary cutter or sharp scissors.

INTERFACING

Fusible tricot.

THREAD

Good-quality cotton or polyester.

NEEDLE

80/12 H.

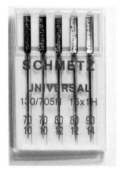

STITCH LENGTH

2.5 mm.

PRESSER FOOT

Standard.

SEAM FINISH

Flat fell. (See #9 on p. 175.)

PRESSING

Cotton setting with steam. No press cloth necessary.

TOPSTITCHING

¼ in. from edge with regular thread. (See #10 on p. 181.)

CLOSURES

Snaps, machine button-holes. (See #1 on p. 182, #11 on p. 184.)

HEM

Double roll ½-in. hem, machine-stitch on blouse. (See #10 on p. 188.) Hand-hem on jacket, pants, or dress. (See #4 on p. 187.)

Cotton damask

FABRIC FACT
While fabric is usually all one color, shiny threads create print on a matte surface.

SUITABLE FOR
Jacket, blouse, tailored pants, straight or semi-full dress.

SEWING TIPS
Easy to sew and press.

Tip: Check the tension on your sewing machine. You don't know how to do that? Try this. Put a different color thread on the top than on the bobbin. Sew for a few inches. If the bobbin color shows on the top side of the fabric, loosen the upper tension by turning the tension knob to a lower number. If the top thread shows on the bottom of the fabric, tighten the tension by turning the tension knob to a higher number.

Cotton Piqué

PRESHRINK

Machine-wash in warm water and machine-dry on regular cycle. If using black piqué, hand-wash in cold water and air-dry. This will maintain the "black" and prevent graying.

LAYOUT

"Without nap" layout, double thickness.

MARKING

Clo-Chalk, tracing wheel, snips in seam allowance.

CUTTING

Rotary cutter or scissors.

INTERFACING

Fuse-Knit on a blouse, Suit Shape on a vest or jacket.

THREAD

Good-quality cotton or polyester.

NEEDLE

80/12 H.

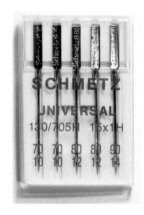

STITCH LENGTH

2.5 mm.

PRESSER FOOT

Standard.

SEAM FINISH

Flat fell or sew with a straight seam, press open, and overlock each side of seam separately. No seam finish if lining. (See #3 on p. 174, #27 on p. 178.)

PRESSING

Cotton setting with steam.

TOPSTITCHING

Not recommended since it detracts from fabric's surface.

CLOSURES

Buttonholes, snaps, and button loops. (See #1 on p. 182, #9 on p. 183, #11 on p. 184.)

HEM

Serge raw edge. Sew by hand or topstitch with double needle. (See #1 and #4 on p. 187.)

Cotton piqué

FABRIC FACT
Cotton piqué is medium-weight cotton with raised, pebbly weave, which looks almost like a small check.

SUITABLE FOR
Vests, jackets, fitted blouses.

SEWING TIPS
Easy to sew.

Tip: If you love a fabric but don't know how much to buy, 2½ yards gives you the option of making pants, a blouse, some skirts, or a simple jacket. Three yards is safer if you like to double fronts on blouses and jackets.

Cotton Shirting

PRESHRINK

Serge crossgrain ends to prevent excess raveling. Machine-wash in warm water and machine-dry on regular temperature. Remove while slightly damp. Iron-dry, stretching slightly in lengthwise direction only. This will prevent puckered seams.

LAYOUT

"Without nap" layout, double thickness.

MARKING

Fabric markers, tracing wheel, clips in seam allowance.

CUTTING

Rotary cutter or scissors.

INTERFACING

Shirtailor or Durapress. Interface both layers of collar and cuffs.

THREAD

Good-quality cotton.

NEEDLE

70/10 H.

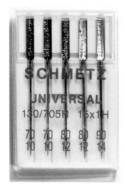

STITCH LENGTH

2.5 mm straight stitch for seams, 1.8 mm for collar points and curves.

PRESSER FOOT

Standard or felling foot.

SEAM FINISH

Flat fell or French. (See #9 and #10 on p. 175.)

PRESSING

Steam iron on cotton setting. For crisp details use spray starch.

TOPSTITCHING

Close to the edge with edge foot or edge-joining foot using a 70/10 HJ needle. (See #3 on p. 180.)

CLOSURES

For buttonholes, use 70/10 HJ with extra-fine thread. (See #1 on p. 182.)

HEM

¼-in. double-fold hem with topstitching. (See #10 on p. 188.) Ease-stitch on curves. (See #8 on p. 188.)

Cotton shirting

FABRIC FACT

Look for very fine weaves in 100% cotton shirting for the most luxurious to wear and finest quality.

SUITABLE FOR

Tailored shirts and pajamas.

SEWING TIPS

Easy to sew.

Tip: Edge stitching is different than topstitching. Edge stitching is used to control an edge. It should be very close to the edge, in matching non-decorative thread, and in a medium stitch length. Edge stitching should not be very visible, unlike topstitching.

Cotton Voile

PRESHRINK
Hand-wash in Ivory flakes. Drip-dry.

LAYOUT
"Without nap" layout, double thickness using new, fine glass-head pins.

MARKING
Fabric markers, pencils, tailor tacks.

CUTTING
Rotary cutter or scissors.

INTERFACING
Self-fabric.

THREAD
Fine machine embroidery cotton.

NEEDLE
60/8 H or 65/9 H.

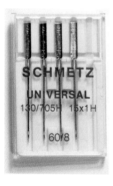

STITCH LENGTH
2.0 mm straight stitch.

PRESSER FOOT
Use single-hole presser foot and single-hole throat plate or switch needle to the far left position for support on three sides. Loosen top tension one-eighth to one-quarter of a turn.

SEAM FINISH
French seams. (See #10 on p. 175.)

PRESSING
Cotton setting with steam. For crispness, use spray starch.

TOPSTITCHING
Close to finished edge. Use edge foot or edge-joining foot for accuracy. (See #3 on p. 180.)

CLOSURES
For buttonholes, use 60/8 H new needle and fine cotton machine embroidery thread to reduce bulk. (See #1 on p. 182.)

HEM
Narrow rolled hem on the serger is a good finish for ruffles. (See #16 on p. 189.) Set cutting width wider to roll more fabric into the stitch. Hand stitches or machine decorative stitches also work well on the hem.

Cotton voile

FABRIC FACT
Cotton voile is slightly crisper than batiste and is used for heirloom dresses or underlining where some crispness is desired.

SUITABLE FOR
Heirloom sewing and underlining. 100% Swiss cotton is preferred on heirloom work because the lace does not lie as flat on the polyester blends and underlining because it breathes.

SEWING TIPS
Staystitching is very important. Do not backstitch. Begin and end with a machine knot or tie threads.

Tip: Interface both sides of a stand-up collar with medium-weight interfacing. Cut all four layers on the bias.

Denim

PRESHRINK

Wash separately since colors bleed. Machine-wash in warm water and machine-dry on regular temperature. Preshrink twice to eliminate all shrinkage. After second drying, remove fabric while still slightly damp and iron-dry. This prevents crease lines formed in the drying stage. If you want a "faded" look, wash and bleach fabric three to five times.

LAYOUT

"Without nap" layout for regular denim and "with nap" layout for brushed denim. Double thickness. Grainline is very important. Off-grain cuts create problems like twisting pants legs.

MARKING

Chalk, fabric markers.

CUTTING

Sharp scissors or rotary cutter.

INTERFACING

Waistbands—Armo Weft; shirts—French fuse or Fuse-Knit.

THREAD

Good-quality polyester or upholstery thread if seams will be under stress.

NEEDLE

90/14 HJ for light weight or 100/16 HJ for heavy weight.

STITCH LENGTH

2.5 mm lighter weight, 3.0 mm heavier weight.

PRESSER FOOT

Regular for seams, roller foot in bulky areas.

SEAM FINISH

Few machines are capable of joining two flat-fell seams at the crotch. Instead, serge one side of the seam allowance, then trim the other. Without turning under, overlap serged seam allowance onto trimmed seam allowance. Topstitch. This forms a fake flat fell that is less bulky and easier to sew. (See #27 on p. 178.)

PRESSING

High-temperature steam iron.

TOPSTITCHING

Lengthen stitch to 3.5 mm and use heavy-duty or upholstery thread ¼ in. from edge. Guterman, YLI, and Signature make colors that match the color and weight used in ready-to-wear jeans. If you can find a double-needle ZWI HJ 40/100, you can topstitch two parallel rows at once on denim. (See #23 and #24 on p. 190.)

CLOSURES

Snaps make the best closures. (See #11 on p. 184.)

HEM

Use heavy-duty or upholstery thread and a 100/16 HJ needle. Roll hem twice at ¾ in. Pound with a tailor's clapper to flatten before stitching. Sew two rows of parallel stitching with a single needle. Only a double-needle ZWI HJ 40/100 is sharp enough for double-needle hemming on denim. (See #16 on p. 189.)

Denim

FABRIC FACT
Denim is the workhorse of cotton fabrics.

SUITABLE FOR
Jeans, bomber jackets, straight skirts, semi-fitted shirt dresses, tailored shirts, upholstery, and pillows. Denim comes in two weights. Lightweight denim is better for shirts and dresses. Heavyweight denim is better for pants, straight skirts, and jackets.

SEWING TIPS
Prevent skipped stitches by holding fabric taut whenever you are machine-sewing or serging as the machine goes through multiple layers.

Tip: Hand-baste the outside edges of a jacket or blouse before you press. You will get a much sharper crease. Don't forget to use silk thread for the basting. Other threads leave a memory.

Faux Leather

PRESHRINK

Mandatory or you will get skipped stitches. Machine-wash in warm water on short cycle and machine-dry on synthetic cycle. On finished garment, leave in dryer only a few minutes. Remove and pull seams taut to remove puckers.

LAYOUT

"Without nap" layout, double thickness. Use fabric in any direction. Use pattern weights.

MARKING

Fabric markers or chalk. Do not use tracing wheel with spokes. This will put holes in the fabric.

CUTTING

Rotary cutter or scissors.

INTERFACING

French Fuse or Fuse-Knit.

THREAD

Good-quality polyester.

NEEDLE

75/11 HS.

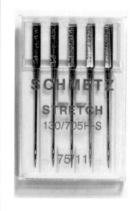

STITCH LENGTH

2.5 mm.

PRESSER FOOT

Teflon foot.

SEAM FINISH

Fake flat fell. (See #27 on p. 178.)

PRESSING

Use a dry iron on high synthetic setting and a press cloth on both sides or fabric will stick to iron.

TOPSTITCHING

Topstitch ¼ in. from finished edge with regular thread and a 3.0 mm stitch. (See #10 on p. 181.)

CLOSURES

For buttonholes, use bound buttonhole or faced opening. (See #6 and #8 on p. 183.) Excellent candidate for invisible zippers, but stabilize seam allowance with fusible knitted tricot. (See #18 on p. 176.)

HEM

Fuse hem with Stitch Witchery or glue with fabric glue. (See #3 on p. 187, #7 on p. 188.)

Tip: To make your own piping from synthetic leather or wool jersey, cut on the crossgrain for maximum stretch. You can prevent the jacket front and facing seam from shortening if piping is hand-basted rather than machine-basted to facing.

Faux leather

FABRIC FACT
This fabric washes beautifully and breathes a little.

SUITABLE FOR
Pants, skirts, jackets, trench coats. Since this fabric has a nice drape, it can be used on straight or slightly full styles. Since the fabric is water-proof, it is excellent for rainwear. It also makes great trim since it stretches a bit; crossgrain leather can be used as "bias trim."

SEWING TIPS
Use paper clips to hold seams together for sewing or pin only in the seam allowance. Since this fabric has a tendency to stick to the body, consider lining with Bemberg rayon "Ambiance." Using a polyester lining will prevent the fabric from breathing at all, making it very hot to wear. For more realistic leather-looking pants, create a seam at the knee. Supple leather skins come in small sizes and cannot accommodate the whole leg.

Faux Suede

PRESHRINK
To soften and create better drape, machine-wash in warm water and detergent, and machine-dry on a low setting with towel and tennis shoe five times. Leave finished garment in dryer for a few minutes only. Remove and pull seams taut to remove puckers.

LAYOUT
"With nap" layout. Pattern pieces can be tilted because the fabric has no real grainline. Pieces can be angled 45 degrees without affecting color shading. Use pattern weights.

MARKING
Fabric markers or snips in seam allowances.

CUTTING
Rotary cutter works the best, but scissors are okay.

INTERFACING
French Fuse or Fuse-Knit.

THREAD
Good-quality polyester.

NEEDLE
75/11 HS or 70/10 HJ for lightweight; 80/12 HJ for heavy weight.

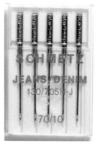

STITCH LENGTH
2.5 mm.

PRESSER FOOT
Walking foot or Teflon foot.

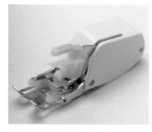

SEAM FINISH
Fake flat fell. (See #27 on p. 178.)

PRESSING
Use a press cloth and steam iron on medium-high temperature. Overpressing can be corrected with steam and a small brush.

TOPSTITCHING
Use 90/14 HS needle and lengthen stitch to 3.5 mm using a decorative or topstitching thread. (See #10 on p. 181.)

CLOSURES
For buttonholes, use 70/10 HJ needle. Use Solvy between presser foot and fabric. Bound buttonholes are attractive. For an even easier buttonhole, fuse facing and garment together with Stitch Witchery in the buttonhole area. Sew a narrow rectangle ¼ in. longer than desired for buttonhole opening on the right side through both layers. Cut slit for buttonhole opening. (See #1 on p. 182, #8 on p. 183, #17 on p. 186.)

HEM
Fuse hem with Stitch Witchery or glue with fabric glue. (See #3 on p. 187.)

Faux suede

FABRIC FACT

This fabric can be somewhat stiff and puffy on the body. Prewashing and machine-drying five times helps to relax it and make it more flattering for garments.

SUITABLE FOR

Home-dec items such as pillows and valances and fashion accessories such as purses, small containers, and belts. Since this is a sturdy, crisp fabric for garment sewing, choose a pattern with straight seams and a boxy silhouette like a jacket, straight skirt, or narrow pants that do not feature fabric drape. Since faux suede doesn't ease well, choose raglan or dolman sleeves.

SEWING TIPS

Use paper clips to hold seams together for sewing.

Tip: Would you like to eliminate the dimple at the end of the dart in gabardine, Ultrasuede, and other difficult-to-press fabrics? Cut a 2-in. square of linen with pinking shears. Place square under the small end of the dart as you sew. Let 1 in. of square protrude off end of dart. Sew dart from fat to skinny end, switching to small stitches ½ in. from dart point. To press, place dart over ham. Linen square fills in the space at the end of the dart. The result is a dart without a dimple. (See #7 on p. 181.)

Gabardine

PRESHRINK

Options: 1) Hold steam iron ½ in. above surface before cutting.
2) Wool gabardine can be hand-washed in the bathtub. Hand-wash with shampoo in cold water twice. Do not wring dry—merely squeeze out water. Spin in no-heat dryer to take out excess moisture. Serge ends together. Stretch if off grain. Air-dry flat. 3) Preshrink at the dry cleaner. 4) If garment is not worn for long periods of time, steam-press to raise diagonal weave.

LAYOUT

"With nap" layout, double thickness.

MARKING

Tailor tacks, tailor's chalk, Clo-Chalk.

CUTTING

Rotary cutter or scissors. Cutting seam allowances ¼ in. wider than normal enables seams to press flatter.

INTERFACING

Hymo Hair Canvas for tailoring, Durapress Sew-In for softer support. Armo Weft does not give a long-term fuse, lifting off of gabardine's surface after several dry cleanings.

THREAD

Good-quality silk, cotton, or polyester.

NEEDLE

80/12 H.

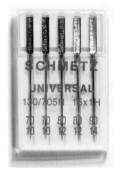

STITCH LENGTH

3.0 mm.

PRESSER FOOT

Standard, loosen top tension slightly.

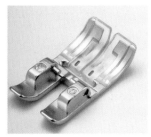

SEAM FINISH

Options: 1) Pressed open and serged separately using woolly nylon on the lower looper. 2) Flat fell. 3) Hong Kong bound. (See #3 on p. 174, #9 on p. 175, #16 on p. 176.)

PRESSING

Press seam as stitched. With seam positioned over a seam roll, seam stick, or half-round to prevent seam allowance show-through on right side, dribble a bead of water in the valley of the seam. Press with steam iron on wool setting. Use no more pressure than the weight of the iron on wrong side. On right side of fabric, position seam over half round. Cover with self-fabric press cloth. Press with steam. Let fabric cool and dry before moving from pressing surface. If fabric becomes overpressed and shines, hold steam iron ½ in. above right side of fabric. Brush with tailor's brush.

TOPSTITCHING

Very close to the sewn edge using edge foot or edge-joining foot as a guide, ¼ in. from the finished edge or hand-picked. (See #1 and #3 on p. 180, #10 on p. 181.)

CLOSURES

For buttonholes, use 70/10 HJ needle and cord to prevent stretching. Rayon thread and a 90/14 HJ needle make incredible buttonholes on this fabric. Snaps are also suitable. (See #5 on p. 182, #11 on p. 184.)

HEM

Hand-sewn or topstitched. (See #4 on p. 187, #10 on p. 188.)

Gabardine

FABRIC FACT
Gabardine is a twill weave
that has a beautiful drape
and is highly wrinkle resistant.
While wool gabardine is the most
common, gabardine also comes
in silk, cotton, and rayon.

SUITABLE FOR
Tailored styles, trench coats, tailored
jackets, tailored pants, straight skirts,
or loose shirts. Styles with drape do
very well in gabardine. Since gabardine
does not ease well, raglan or dolman
sleeves look more professional unless
you are a very experienced sewer.

SEWING TIPS
Very easy to sew but not so easy
to get a good press.

Tip: If a fabric is
very difficult to
ease such as wool
gabardine,
remove all but
half of ease or try
running an ease
line all around the
sleeve, from
underarm to
underarm.

Hemp Cloth

PRESHRINK

While this fabric can be machine-washed and dried on the gentle cycle, it is very difficult to press. Darker colors lose dye. Experiment with a sample. If you decide to dry-clean, preshrink by holding steam iron ½ in. above fabric surface.

LAYOUT

"Without nap" layout, double thickness.

MARKING

Clo-Chalk, fabric markers, tailor's wax.

CUTTING

This fabric is rather difficult to cut. Use long, sharp scissors to get better leverage or a rotary cutter.

INTERFACING

Except for a jacket, fabric has enough body so that interfacing is not necessary. For jackets, use Armo Weft.

THREAD

Good-quality cotton or polyester.

NEEDLE

90/14 H.

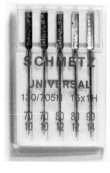

STITCH LENGTH

2.5 mm.

PRESSER FOOT

Standard.

SEAM FINISH

Sew seam, overlock together, and press to one side or flat fell. (See #4 on p. 174, #9 on p. 175.) On unlined jacket, finish seams with double-fold bias. (See #20 on p. 177.)

PRESSING

Use lots of steam on high heat, linen setting. Use spray starch to crispen details such as collars and pockets.

TOPSTITCHING

Results are excellent. Close to finished edge or ¼ in. from finished edge. Edge foot or edge-joining foot is helpful here. Lengthen stitch to 3.5 mm. (See #3 on p. 180, #10 on p. 181.)

CLOSURES

For buttonholes, use 70/10 HJ needle and fine machine embroidery thread to reduce bulk. Widen, don't lengthen, buttonhole stitch if possible. (See #4 on p. 182.)

HEM

Hand-hem or topstitch with double needle. (See #1 and #4 on p. 187.)

Hemp cloth

FABRIC FACT
This sturdy plant-fiber fabric is similar to linen except that it doesn't wrinkle as much; the wrinkles are larger and tend to hang out.

SUITABLE FOR
Medium weight is suitable for oversized shirts, wrap skirts, and loose dresses. Heavy weight is suitable for jacket, vests, and jeans. This fabric makes a great canvas for decorative stitching.

SEWING TIPS
Easy to sew.

Tip: When doing decorative stitching, use two strands of thread in the needle if you want your design to be filled in closer.

Insulation

PRESHRINK

Not necessary. Machine-wash in warm water, machine-dry on cool setting only. Thinsulate can only be dry-cleaned if you label your garment "Thinsulate" so the dry cleaner will not press it (this fabric melts when pressed).

LAYOUT

Can be cut lengthwise or crosswise, double layer. Cut from lining pieces. Pattern weights work better than pins.

MARKING

Due to the deep pile, it is difficult to get markings to show up. Since the insulation will never be seen, marking does not have to come out. Felt-tip marker shows up the best.

CUTTING

Scissors or large rotary cutter.

INTERFACING

Not necessary.

THREAD

Good-quality polyester or cotton.

NEEDLE

Select a needle to suit the fabric you are underlining.

STITCH LENGTH

Long, wide zigzag (3.5 mm width and length).

PRESSER FOOT

Standard.

SEAM FINISH

Finger-press seam allowances open and topstitch ¼ in. away from seam on each side to decrease bulk. Trim away excess seam allowance. (See #13 on p. 176.)

PRESSING

Finger-press only.

TOPSTITCHING

Not appropriate.

CLOSURES

Choose closures according to fashion fabric.

HEM

Attach lining to fashion fabric at hem.

Insulation

FABRIC FACT

Thermal insulation is available under the brand names Thinsulate and Lite Loft in different weights to suit various climates and activities. Thinsulate claims equal warmth with half the bulk.

SUITABLE FOR

Interlining for warmth.

SEWING TIPS

Cut insulation the same size as the lining. Zigzag to lining pieces. Treat combined pieces as one during the remainder of construction.

Knits, Stable

PRESHRINK

When using cotton knits, buy an additional ¼ yard for every 2 yards cut. Fabric has progressive shrinkage, which means it must be machine-washed in warm water and dried at regular temperature two times before cutting out. Preshrink wool knits by holding a steam iron ½ in. above the surface. Dry-clean completed wool garment.

LAYOUT

Check for runs, snags, and if lengthwise crease is still visible after preshrinking. If so, crease is permanent. Cut around it. If selvage is crooked, follow rib in fabric for straight of grain. "With nap" layout, double or single thickness, as many fabrics shade differently in opposite direction. Use greatest stretch of the knit around the body.

MARKING

Fabric markers, Clo-Chalk, snips at notches.

CUTTING

Rotary cutter or scissors, pattern weights.

INTERFACING

Fusible weft insertion, Flex Weave, or Whisper Weft.

THREAD

Good-quality polyester is the best choice since it has some stretch. Wind bobbin slowly.

NEEDLE

75/11 HS.

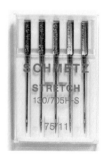

STITCH LENGTH

Tiny zigzag (0.5 mm width, 2.5 mm length) or stretch stitch.

PRESSER FOOT

Standard.

SEAM FINISH

Sew seams first with a tiny zigzag or stretch stitch. Reduce pressure on presser foot or keep finger pushing into fabric behind presser foot to prevent stretching. Sew seams with a 3- or 4-thread overlock with woolly nylon on the loopers. Use differential feed or your finger behind the presser foot to prevent stretching. (See #8 on p. 175, #21 on p. 177.) Use triple stitch in areas of stress such as crotch and underarm seams. (See #6 on p. 174.)

PRESSING

Steam iron on cotton setting. On wool double-knit, reduce iron temperature to wool setting. Do not over press or it will look flat and shiny.

TOPSTITCHING

Lengthen stitch to 3.0 mm and topstitch ¼ in. from finished edge. (See #10 on p. 181.)

CLOSURES

Stabilize buttonhole area with lengthwise grain of interfacing parallel to buttonhole. For buttonholes, use 70/10 HJ and fine thread, using Solvy between the presser foot and the knit. Sew corded buttonholes to prevent stretching. (See #5 on p. 182.) Stabilize zipper seam allowances with ½-in. strips of fusible interfacing that are pinked to avoid a ridge. (See #18 on p. 176.) Hand-picked zippers look the classiest. (See #5 on p. 180.)

HEM

Double-needle ZWI stretch with woolly nylon hand-wrapped on the bobbin and Teflon or roller presser foot to prevent stretching as you topstitch. Flatlock only on non-bulky knits with a 2-thread flatlock stitch. (See #1 and #2 on p. 187.)

Knits, stable

FABRIC FACT
Good examples of stable knits are wool double-knit, polyester double-knit, and ribbing, where both sides of the fabric look the same. Look for knits that when fabric is stretched on the crossgrain return to original size when released.

SUITABLE FOR
Unstructured jackets, pull-on pants, cardigans, T-shirt dresses, gored or wrap skirts.

SEWING TIPS
Stabilize neck, shoulders, and waistline seams with ¼-in. clear elastic using a walking foot. Do not stretch fabric as you sew since this results in wavy seams. Eliminate facings whenever possible. Overlock raw edge. Turn under using staystitching line to help you. Topstitch with the double-needle ZWI stretch 4.0 mm width with woolly nylon hand-wrapped on bobbin. (See #8 on p. 181.)

Tip: Never put anything black in the dryer unless you prefer grayed-out color.

Lace

PRESHRINK

Most laces are washable, but be sure to preshrink by hand-washing in warm water and air-drying. Even polyester lace can shrink. If you plan to dry-clean lace garment. Steam the wrong side of the lace using a towel underneath the lace to prevent flattening design. Never touch lace with the iron. Hold iron ½ in. above the surface.

LAYOUT

Spread lace on a contrasting cutting surface so you can see motifs. Position pattern pieces so prominent motifs are balanced. Try to position scalloped edged at neck or hem. If this is not possible, scalloped edge can be cut off and reapplied after garment is completed. "With nap" layout, single layer. If lace doesn't have definite motifs that need matching, the lace can simply be cut out along the pattern cutting lines.

MARKING

Tailor tacks or thread tracing. Thread-trace motif outlines and actual seamlines to extend beyond seamline for accurate seam overlap.

CUTTING

Flower-head pins do not get lost in the fabric. Cut out along motif line or pattern cutting lines if lace has allover pattern that doesn't require matching. Eliminate facing whenever possible by using edge of lace or binding with bias satin or bridal tulle.

INTERFACING

Tulle gives body and retains transparency. Underlining in one tone darker than your skin looks the most natural.

THREAD

Good-quality cotton or polyester.

NEEDLE

75/11 HS.

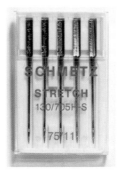

STITCH LENGTH

Short, narrow zigzag (0.5 mm width, 1.5 mm length).

PRESSER FOOT

Presser foot with flattest bottom.

SEAM FINISH

To preserve prominent motif without losing motif design, superimpose seamline of one piece onto seamline of another. Zigzag over prominent motif on top piece. Trim away excess lace on bottom and top so that pattern is single layer and motif uninterrupted. On conventional seams, finish with Seams Great or satin binding in a Hong Kong finish. No seam finish is necessary if garment is lined. (See #16 and #19 on p. 176.)

PRESSING

Cover pressing surface with towel to avoid flattening lace. Hold steam iron ½ in. above fabric. Steam and pat flat. Never touch lace with an iron.

TOPSTITCHING

Not recommended.

CLOSURES

Consider alternate closures like button loops. (See #13 on p. 184.)

HEM

Since lace can be cut apart without raveling, consider using the decorative edge of lace as a hemline. It could be cut off at the beginning and applied later by hand. For lace without decorative edge, finish raw edge with Seams Great and hand-sew. (See #14 on p. 189, #28 on p. 191.)

Lace

FABRIC FACT
Nylon lace is the least expensive and good for pretesting a garment that will be made in a re-embroidered or beaded lace.

SUITABLE FOR
Simple silhouettes with minimum seams to showcase fabric. Pretest pattern. Seams are permanent!

SEWING TIPS
Stabilize shoulders and waistline seams with stay-tape or ¼-in.-wide selvage cut from lightweight lining fabric. On very fine lace, use Solvy between the lace and feed dogs to prevent the lace from being pulled down into the bobbin thread hole. (See #26 on p. 177.) On stretch lace, consider lining with bathing suit lining—it stretches!

Tip: Since lingerie fabric comes in a wider variety of colors than lace, dye the lace to your liking. Match lace to lingerie fabric.

Lamé

PRESHRINK

Hand-wash then air-dry tissue lamé. Machine-wash tricot-backed lamé in warm water on delicate cycle and air-dry.

LAYOUT

"With nap" layout, double thickness. Fabric snags easily, so remove jewelry when working on it. Tricot lamé can be cut on any grain; tissue lamé is more particular.

MARKING

Fabric markers, snips in seam, no waxed chalk.

CUTTING

Rotary cutter or scissors and glass-head pins. Ravels like crazy. Seal edges with Fray Check, which will bleed and darken fabric ¼ in. into seam allowance. Serging pulls off fabric. If the fabric is synthetic, a hot stencil cutter cuts and seals at the same time.

INTERFACING

French Fuse or Fuse-Knit. Consider fusing all cut-out pieces to make fabric easier to handle and less scratchy, a must for appliqué. Test iron temperature on a scrap piece.

THREAD

Good-quality polyester.

NEEDLE

70/10 HJ. Needles dull quickly on a conventional machine or serger, so have plenty on hand. Watch sewing closely as the dull needles will snag the fabric.

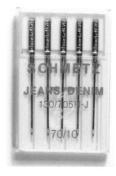

STITCH LENGTH

2.5 mm.

PRESSER FOOT

Use straight stitch foot or flattest bottom presser foot you have. If you don't have these feet, use needle in far left position, which gives support on three sides.

SEAM FINISH

Seams Great and zigzag stitch or small French seams. (See #10 on p. 175, #19 on p. 176.) Serging pulls right off fabric.

PRESSING

Dry iron on synthetic setting with press cloth.

TOPSTITCHING

Not recommended.

CLOSURES

Buttonholes not recommended. Consider alternate closures like button loops and frogs. (See #9 on p. 183, #12 on p. 184.)

HEM

Rolled hem on serger. Widen the bite and lengthen the stitch so that more fabric is rolled under to prevent hem from pulling off fabric. (See #16 on p. 189.)

Lamé

FABRIC FACT
Contains copper, aluminum, or gold and is available in about a dozen colors. Most easily found are tricot-backed lamé and tissue lamé.

SUITABLE FOR
Appliqué, trim, loose tops. Allow enough ease. Fabric is fragile and tears easily.

SEWING TIPS
Pull fabric with equal pressure from front and back as you sew.

Tip: To reduce stretch when using polyester thread, loosen the top and bobbin tension.

Linen

PRESHRINK

Fabric will wrinkle less if you press first to set the formaldehyde. Machine-washing in warm water and machine-drying at regular temperature with detergent and a towel will give the linen a slightly brushed appearance and softer hand. Add 1 tablespoon of bleach to white and off-white colors to soften more. Prewashed fabric will wrinkle less. You will also lose some color. Press well before layout. If you prefer a very crisp look or do not want any color change, preshrinking is not necessary, but the garment will require dry cleaning.

LAYOUT

"Without nap" layout, double thickness.

MARKING

Fabric markers, tracing wheel, snips in the seam allowance, Clo-Chalk.

CUTTING

Rotary cutter or scissors. On handkerchief linen, the lightest weight in linen, cut blouse fronts double and no facings. This will give more coverage in front and eliminate edge of facing show-through.

INTERFACING

French Fuse or Fuse-Knit. On handkerchief linen, interface only with itself.

THREAD

Good-quality cotton or polyester.

NEEDLE

70/10 H handkerchief weight; 80/12 H for other weights.

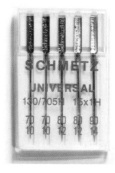

STITCH LENGTH

2.5 mm.

PRESSER FOOT

Standard.

SEAM FINISH

Flat fell or bind separately with narrow double-fold bias. (See #9 on p. 175, #20 on p. 177.)

PRESSING

High temperature with steam on the right side. Spritz with water.

TOPSTITCHING

For beautiful topstitching on heavier weights use Buttonhole Twist on the top, regular thread on the bobbin, and an N needle. Use edge foot or edge-joining foot as guide.

CLOSURES

For buttonholes, use 70/10 HJ and fine machine embroidery thread. Loosen top tension slightly. Linen is a great candidate for snaps. Use 1-in. circle of stiff interfacing for snap support. (See #1 on p. 182, #11 on p. 184.)

HEM

For a beautiful hem-stitch finish, like the one on linen napkins, use a double-needle ZWI-HO, which has an H needle on the right side and a wing needle on the left side to create a hole. Double-fold machine hem on shirts. On jackets, interface hemline with bias-cut strips 1 in. wider than hem of fusible or non-fusible interfacing. Hand-hem on jackets, pants, and skirts. (See #13 and #16 on p. 189.)

Linen

FABRIC FACT
Linen is a crisp fabric that doesn't drape. The biggest mistake people make with linen is using the wrong weight for their project, such as heavy-weight linen for a blouse or tissue weight for pants. Observe linen weights used in ready-to-wear and choose the weight for your project accordingly.

SUITABLE FOR
Dresses, pants, loose shirts, jackets.

SEWING TIPS
To reduce wrinkling, consider fusing the entire garment with fusible knitted tricot. This does add warmth since the fabric cannot breathe as well. Another option is to underline with silk organza. While this reduces wrinkles slightly, using fusible tricot reduces wrinkles the most.

Tip: Comfortable, soft linen can be created by pretreating fabric by running it three times through the washer and dryer with detergent.

Microfiber

PRESHRINK

Machine-wash in warm water, machine-dry at normal temperature. Use only liquid fabric softener. Dryer sheets leave oily spots. On completed garment, remove from dryer before bone-dry, and pull seams taut to prevent puckering. Air-dry.

LAYOUT

"With nap" layout, double thickness on grain. Cut lightweight microfibers 10% off-grain to avoid puckered seams.

MARKING

Clo-Chalk or fabric markers.

CUTTING

Sharp scissors or rotary cutter.

INTERFACING

SofBrush, Soft 'n' Silky, or Touch o' Gold, which bond at low temperatures (a high-temperature iron will melt fabric).

THREAD

Fine machine embroidery.

NEEDLE

60/8 H, 65/9 H, 70/10 HM. Have several on hand because fabric dulls needles quickly.

STITCH LENGTH

1.5 mm straight stitch.

PRESSER FOOT

Flattest bottom presser foot.

SEAM FINISH

On lightweight microfibers press open and pink or 2-thread overlock each side of seam allowance with super-fine serger thread such as Janome overlock polyester thread #80. (See #2 and #3 on p. 174.) On heavier microfibers, 3- or 4-thread overlock can be used with normal-weight thread.

PRESSING

Dry, moderate-heat iron. Press seam as stitched before pressing open. Use a press cloth when ironing on the right side. Press over rounded seam stick to prevent serger stitches from making ridges on the right side.

TOPSTITCHING

Very close to edge. Farther away causes ripples. (See #2 on p. 180.) Edge foot or edge-joining foot is helpful here.

CLOSURES

For buttonholes, use a 70/10 HJ with fine machine embroidery thread and Solvy between fabric and feed dogs. (See #1 on p. 182.)

HEM

No double-needle top-stitching since puckers often form between rows. For the most invisible hems, fuse with Stitch Witchery Ultra Light, which doesn't come off in washer and dryer if you used enough steam for long-term fusing. Hand-stitching is second choice. (See #3 and #4 on p. 187.)

Microfiber

FABRIC FACT
Microfiber is the finest-quality polyester at 200 threads per inch. Microfiber comes in different weights, with the heavier weight giving the best seam results. Fabric might be labeled peach skin, micro twill, or micro sandwashed. This fabric is very drapey, but does not breathe.

SUITABLE FOR
Loose unstructured styles with minimum seams such as full coats, tailored pants, full wrap skirts in medium weight, nightgowns or pajamas in lightweight. Fabric does not ease well, so raglan or dolman sleeves give better results. Since it is difficult to achieve a sharp press, choose style accordingly.

SEWING TIPS
Place needle in the far left position to reduce puckering and use the flattest bottom presser foot. Or use a single-hole throat plate.

Tip: On fine fabrics, a very small needle causes the least fabric distortion, thereby eliminating puckered seams.

Mohair

PRESHRINK
Hold steam iron ½ in. above fabric.

LAYOUT
"With nap" layout, pile down, single thickness.

MARKING
Tailor tacks.

CUTTING
Rotary cutter or scissors, pattern weights.

INTERFACING
Organza or Verishape on the bias for crisper detailing.

THREAD
Silk machine twist or good-quality cotton.

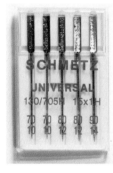

NEEDLE
70/10 H or 80/12 H.

STITCH LENGTH
2.5 mm straight stitch.

PRESSER FOOT
Walking.

SEAM FINISH
Use stabilizing organza strip to bind seams together. (See #15 on p. 176.) Render seams almost invisible by brushing pressed-open seams against the nap from the right side with a toothbrush.

PRESSING
Cover pressing surface with Velva board. On the wrong side, press only in the seam allowance with the tip of a dry iron on medium temperature. No pressing on the right side. Details such as pockets and lapels can be flattened with the right side against the Velva board. Cover mohair with press cloth. Press with steam on the wool setting. A tailor's clapper can be used gently.

TOPSTITCHING
Not necessary, but can help flatten edges if done ⅜ in. from finished edge. Walking foot should be used when topstitching. (See #9 on p. 181.) Loosen top tension slightly.

CLOSURES
Consider other buttonhole options such as a faced opening, button loops, or openings in a seam. If you are an expert, face front edge with grosgrain. Make buttonhole through grosgrain and mohair. (See #6, #7, #9, and #10 on p. 183.)

HEM
Hand-hem. (See #4 on p. 187.)

Mohair

FABRIC FACT
Mohair is made from the soft silky hair of the Angora goat.

SUITABLE FOR
Unlined sweater, coat, or jacket. This fabric makes a terrific travel garment because it is lightweight, warm, and never wrinkles. A wonderful lap robe can be made with 1½ yards.

SEWING TIPS
Sew in the direction of the pile. To stabilize seams and prevent them from stretching, sew with a 2-in. strip of organza between the presser foot and the mohair. Underlining is not recommended because mohair will sag over the underlining in time. Lining is optional but it must hang free at the hem.

Tip: Since warp and weft threads shrink differently, fabric for any garment that will be cut on the bias must be preshrunk.

Polyester Silky

PRESHRINK

Not necessary. Completed garment can be hand- or machine-washed in warm water. Air-dry. Machine-drying causes too much static electricity.

LAYOUT

Cut on the crossgrain or the bias to prevent puckered seams. If fabric will be pleated, cut on lengthwise grain since pleat will hide any seam puckering.

MARKING

Fabric markers or snips in the seam allowance.

CUTTING

Rotary cutter or scissors.

INTERFACING

Sew-in or low-temperature fusible interfacings.

THREAD

Fine machine embroidery.

NEEDLE

70/10 HM or 70/10 HJ.

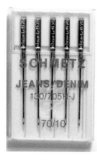

STITCH LENGTH

2.0 mm straight stitch.

PRESSER FOOT

Straight stitch presser foot or use flattest bottom presser foot and switch needle to the far left position.

SEAM FINISH

French seam. (See #10 on p. 175.)

PRESSING

Medium-temperature steam iron. Test sample.

TOPSTITCHING

Close to the edge helps flatten edges. Edge foot helps here. (See #3 on p. 180.)

CLOSURES

Buttonholes using 70/10 HJ needles and fine machine embroidery thread or thread loops. (See #1 on p. 182, #9 on p. 183.)

HEM

Double fold ¼-in. hem by machine. (See #10 on p. 188.)

Polyester silky

FABRIC FACT

While polyester silky is very seductive on the bolt, it is difficult to get seams that don't pucker unless you cut fabric on the cross-grain or bias. Polyester silky is a good candidate to have pleated since polyester will hold pleats indefinitely. Polyester is warm to wear.

SUITABLE FOR

Blouses, nightgowns, and pleated skirts.

SEWING TIPS

Use taut sewing technique of pulling the fabric with equal pressure from both directions.

Tip: To prevent fabric from shifting when making buttonholes, position a small strip of fusible web between the facing and garment in the buttonhole area. The web locks fabrics together during this crucial process.

Puckered Fabrics

PRESHRINK
Not necessary.

LAYOUT
"With nap" layout, single layer.

MARKING
Clo-Chalk or safety pins.

CUTTING
Rotary cutter or scissors. Use pattern weights; pins will tear tissue. Cut and sew 1-in. seam allowances to keep elastic threads from working out as the seam is sewn.

INTERFACING
Silk organza. No fusible interfacing. Stabilize neck and shoulders with narrow, clear elastic. Prestretch elastic once before using. Do not stretch elastic as you apply it; merely lay it on the fabric and stitch through as you are seaming. Lining is not necessary but if desired use swimsuit lining or Lycra in areas where stretch is needed. If fabric is used only for textural effect and no stretch is needed, hand-baste to cotton batiste.

THREAD
Good-quality polyester or cotton.

NEEDLE
70/10 H.

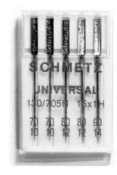

STITCH LENGTH
Narrow zigzag (0.5 mm width, 2.5 mm length).

PRESSER FOOT
Walking foot.

SEAM FINISH
Small zigzag stitch with seam allowances serged separately. (See #3 on p. 174.)

PRESSING
Cover pressing surface with towel and press with low-temperature steam iron. An iron that is too warm will melt elastic threads. Finger-press after steaming.

TOPSTITCHING
Not recommended. Hand-picking close to edge can help flatten seam. (See #1 on p. 180.)

CLOSURES
Invisible zippers, button loops, frogs. (See #9 on p. 183, #12 on p. 184.)

HEM
Serge raw hem edge. Do not allow hem edge to stretch. Use differential feed or push fabric into the back of the presser foot as you serge, just as you would for easing. Turn hem under ½ in. Hand-sew, stretch fabric between every fourth stitch and knot. (See #4 on p. 187.)

Puckered fabrics

FABRIC FACT
The three-dimensional effect in a
puckered fabric is created by
elasticized threads on the fabric
back.

SUITABLE FOR
Details such as collars or
pocket flaps, part of the
garment like the bodice
of an empire-styled
dress, bustier, vest,
simply styled fitted
top, short bolero
jacket, or long
body-conscious
dresses in which
the side seams must be
stabilized with narrow
clear elastic.

SEWING TIPS
To eliminate all hassles and
seam stretching in dealing
with this fabric, sew with
paper strips between the
presser foot and the
fabric and the fabric
and the feed dogs.
Push fabric into
presser foot.
Tear off paper.
Face neckline,
armholes, and
front edge with
lightly inter-
faced non-
puckered
fabric.

Tip: When
sewing over
any elastic
other than
narrow clear
elastic, use a
ball-point
needle to
prevent elas-
tic threads
from damage
and coming
through to the
right side of
the fabric.

Rayon Challis

PRESHRINK

Machine-wash in cold water, on short cycle in Ivory liquid, and machine-dry on permanent press.

LAYOUT

"Without nap" layout, double thickness.

MARKING

Clo-Chalk, tailor tacks, tracing wheel.

CUTTING

Scissors or rotary cutter.

INTERFACING

French Fuse or Fuse-Knit

THREAD

Fine machine embroidery.

NEEDLE

70/10 HJ or 70/10 HM, new needle only. Needle will snag fabric if dull.

STITCH LENGTH

2.5 mm straight stitch.

PRESSER FOOT

Standard.

SEAM FINISH

Flat fell or serged separately with fine serger thread and pressed open. (See #3 on p. 174.)

PRESSING

Steam iron on medium temperature. Since some dye may transfer in pressing, use a disposable press cloth like a paper towel. Some fabrics need to cool before moving on the pressing surface or wrinkles will develop.

TOPSTITCHING

Beautiful results near the finished edge or ¼ in. in from finished edge using edge foot or edge-joining foot. (See #3 on p. 180, #10 on p. 181.)

CLOSURES

For machine buttonholes use 70/10 HJ needle and fine thread. (See #1 on p. 182.)

HEM

Serge or Hong Kong finish raw edge. Turn up 1 in. Hand-hem. (See #4 on p. 187, #13 on p. 189.)

Rayon challis

FABRIC FACT
Not all rayons are created equal. Imported rayons are superior to the domestic ones in that they do not wrinkle as much. Challis is a fabric friend that works in most styles, is flattering to the body, and is also comfortable to wear.

SUITABLE FOR
Full pants, full or A-line skirts, and semi-fitted or full dresses.

SEWING TIPS
Easy to sew.

Rayon Crepe

PRESHRINK
Hold steam iron ½ in. above fabric. Dry-clean completed garment when necessary.

LAYOUT
"With nap" layout, double thickness.

MARKING
Tailor's chalk or snips in seam allowance.

CUTTING
Rotary cutter or scissors. Use sharp pins in seam allowances only.

INTERFACING
Weft insertion or Flex Weave.

THREAD
Good-quality cotton or polyester.

NEEDLE
70/10 H.

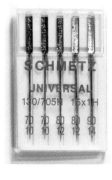

STITCH LENGTH
2.5 mm straight stitch.

PRESSER FOOT
Standard.

SEAM FINISH
Serged separately and pressed open or French seams on blouses. (See #3 on p. 174, #10 on p. 175.)

PRESSING
Medium-temperature steam iron using a press cloth or Teflon iron shoe.

TOPSTITCHING
Close to the edge using edge foot or edge-joining foot. Hand-picking is very attractive ¼ in. from edge, with stitches ¼ in. apart. (See #1 on p. 180.)

CLOSURES
For buttonholes, use 70/10 HJ and fine machine embroidery thread to reduce bulk. If possible move rows of buttonhole stitches closer together. (See #1 on p. 182.)

HEM
Finish raw edge with Hong Kong finish or serger. Turn up 1-in. hem. Blind-hem stitch by machine, hand-stitch, or topstitch with double needle. (See #1, #4, and #6 on p. 187.)

Rayon crepe

FABRIC FACT
While this fabric drapes beautifully and eases well, it is also prone to wrinkles. Consider underlining in cotton batiste or pima cotton.

SUITABLE FOR
Because this fabric is so drapey, it is great for full blouses, full skirts, full pants, and luxurious jacket linings.

SEWING TIPS
For long side seams, use regular presser foot and tiny zigzag (0.5 mm width and 2.5 mm length) with standard presser foot to allow seams to relax as the fabric relaxes.

Tip: Sulky rayon thread creates beautiful topstitching. Use rayon thread on top only, regular thread on the bobbin. Use an **HE** needle. Lengthen stitch. Include ends in seam or tie off threads at underside.

Ripstop

PRESHRINK

Not necessary. Completed garment can be warm-water washed and machine-dried on perma press cycle. Straighten ends with T-square. Trim off selvages, which would cause seam puckering later.

LAYOUT

Store fabric on a roll. "Without nap" layout, single thickness if using stencil cutter and double thickness for rotary cutter or scissors. Pin only in the seam allowances or use pattern weights.

MARKING

Chalk or snips in seam allowance.

CUTTING

If you use a hot stencil cutter and cut single fabric thickness, fabric can be cut and sealed in one operation. Rotary cutter and scissors are also suitable. Seal edges with a candle flame right after cutting to prevent raveling.

INTERFACING

Sew-in interfacing like Durapress behind zippers or snaps or low-temperature fusibles.

THREAD

Cotton-wrapped polyester or spun nylon.

NEEDLE

70/10 HM or 70/10 HJ.

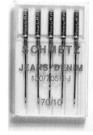

STITCH LENGTH

2.5 mm.

PRESSER FOOT

Teflon or walking foot.

SEAM FINISH

If you did not use a stencil cutter to cut, seal edges quickly with candle flame. Seam with 4-thread overlock. If desired, pull seams to one side and topstitch or sew French seams and then topstitch. (See #5 and #10 on p. 175.)

PRESSING

Medium-temperature iron with steam.

TOPSTITCHING

Seams and details can be topstitched at ⅛ in. to flatten. (See #2 on p. 180.)

CLOSURES

Nylon cord and nylon toggles will not melt in dryer. Or use Velcro or coil zippers, which are self mending. With snaps, use a layer of non-fusible interfacing between fabric layers or snaps will pull away from the fabric. (See #11 on p. 184, #19 on p. 186.)

HEM

Narrow casing and drawstring in shock cord or elastic or ¾-in. double-rolled machine hem. (See #16 on p. 189, #31 on p. 192.)

Ripstop

FABRIC FACT
Ripstop is a lightweight wind-resistant nylon,
more wind resistant than nylon taffeta. Some
ripstops have a durable water-repellent finish that
makes them water repellent as well. Ripstop does
not breathe.

SUITABLE FOR
Lightweight jackets, ponchos, and wind pants.

SEWING TIPS
Use taut sewing, pulling with equal pressure from
front and back. Slower sewing gives more control
over the fabric. If you want a truly water-tight
garment, seal seams with seam-sealant glue.

Tip: Don't sew
over pins. When
the machine is
forced to jump
over a pin, the
stitch is weak-
ened, causing an
area of the seam
to be susceptible
to breaks.

Satin

PRESHRINK

Prewash in warm water and mild detergent without water softener; line dry. This eliminates skipped stitches caused by chemical residue. Completed garment can be hand-washed and line-dried. If static is a problem, spray with Static Guard.

LAYOUT

Double thickness, "with nap" layout. Shiny fabrics shade differently in different directions.

MARKING

Make snips in the seam allowance or use Clo-Chalk. Don't use fabric markers—they bleed into fabric and are hard to remove—or waxed chalk—it leaves spots.

CUTTING

Sharp scissors or rotary cutter.

INTERFACING

Silk organza. Fusible interfacing causes puckers and gives a stiff, board-like appearance to the fabric. Underlining with organza is recommended since the only way to hem invisibly is to attach hem to underlining.

THREAD

Cotton or silk fine machine embroidery.

NEEDLE

70/10 H.

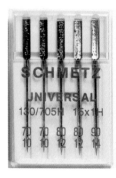

STITCH LENGTH

2.0 mm straight stitch.

PRESSER FOOT

Straight stitch foot, or move needle to the far left position to give support on three sides. Flat underside of the straight stitch foot holds slippery fabrics against feed dogs, reducing puckered seams and skipped stitches.

SEAM FINISH

French seams or serged separately and pressed open. (See #3 on p. 174, #10 on p. 175.)

PRESSING

Dry iron on synthetic setting. Don't use too much pressure as this fabric over presses easily.

TOPSTITCHING

Hand-picking is the best choice. Or machine topstitch close to the finished edge using edge foot or edge-joining foot. (See #3 on p. 180.)

CLOSURES

For buttonholes, use 70/10 HJ and fine embroidery thread to reduce bulk. (See #1 on p. 182.)

HEM

Options: 1) Hem stitching can only be invisible if garment is underlined. Attach hem to underlining. 2) Serged rolled hem with woolly nylon on both loopers, using a longer and wider serger stitch. Move the cutting blade away from needle a bit to allow more fabric to be rolled into hem. Topstitched hems tend to pucker. (See #16 on p. 189.)

Satin

FABRIC FACT
While all satins have a sheen, satins of different fiber content differ in drapability and stitch performance. Rayon is the drapiest, silk is the next, and polyester the least. Both rayon and silk give better stitch results than polyester. Polyester and rayon tend to water-spot, while silk does not. Satin is most often used for bridal or dressy-occasion garments.

SUITABLE FOR
Blouses, full dresses, and coat linings. Use polyester satin only if you are cold natured as it does not breathe.

SEWING TIPS
Sew tautly, pulling fabric from front and back with equal pressure as you sew.

Tip: Puckered seams reduce the value of the finished garment. Use a brand new fine needle for satin.

Sequins

PRESHRINK

Not necessary; store on a roll.

LAYOUT

Before you start, place sheets under cutting table and machine table. This will make clean up much easier. Single layer layout, with pattern pieces placed with the sequin nap *down*, even if this means laying the pieces on the crossgrain. Use pattern weights. Pins are useless here.

MARKING

Tailor tacks or safety pins.

CUTTING

Allow for 1-in. seam allowances. Cut out with old scissors. Sequins will nick the blades. Cut facings in coordinating smooth fabric.

INTERFACING

Sew-in interfacing only like Durapress. No fusibles.

THREAD

Good-quality cotton or polyester.

NEEDLE

90/14 H or 100/16 H. Have plenty, as sequins dull needles.

STITCH LENGTH

3.0 mm.

PRESSER FOOT

Zipper foot.

SEAM FINISH

Finger-press open. Hand-whip to back side of fabric. (See #25 on p. 177.)

PRESSING

Pressing will tarnish the sequins. Finger-press only.

TOPSTITCHING

Not recommended. Hand-picking close to seam can help flatten seam. (See #1 on p. 180.)

CLOSURES

Bias loops made from a coordinating smooth shiny fabric such as satin lining or silk charmeuse. (See #9 on p. 183.) Hand-picked zippers are suitable for fitted garments. (See #19 on p. 186.)

HEM

Face hems in skirts or dresses with a smooth woven fabric or the sequins will run your hose. (See #19 on p. 190.)

Sequins

FABRIC FACT

Allow three times longer to
work on sequins than any
other fabric.

SUITABLE FOR

Simple collarless jackets, tops,
straight skirts, or strapless dresses.
Stick to simple styling: Avoid gathers, pleats, and pockets.

SEWING TIPS

Option 1: Pull sequins out of seam allowances. Do not cut threads. Save some
loose sequins. Using a zipper foot,
staystitch along the seamline. Just outside of
the seamline on the seam allowance, run a
line of Fray Check or clear glue right next to
the staystitch line. This stabilizes the thread
that holds sequins to the fabric. Sew seams
along staystitching line. Using the zipper foot
allows you to sew right next to your seamline with the zipper foot flat in the seam
allowance. Replace damaged sequins or bald
spots near seamline. Option 2: If taking the
sequins out of the seam allowances is just too
much hassle for you, Karen Howland sug-
gests folding back seam allowances on each
side of the seam with folds butting. Join by
sewing seams by hand with the ladder stitch.
Marry sequins on top side by letting sequins
overlap one another, which forces the seam
allowances open. If you use this method, use
a stable lining sewn just a bit smaller than the
sequin fabric to take the stress off of the
seams. (See #38 on p. 179.)

Tip: Carry with you at all times
fabric swatches of garments
you have made or garments in
progress. You never know when
you will see that perfect shoe
or great pair of earrings.
Matching up with fabric
swatches can eliminate a bad
choice or reinforce a good
purchase decision.

Silk Brocade

PRESHRINK
Not necessary. Dry-clean completed garment.

LAYOUT
"With nap" layout, double layer.

MARKING
Fabric pens, Clo-Chalk, tailor tacks.

CUTTING
Sharp scissors or rotary cutter, then overlock each piece separately.

INTERFACING
French Fuse, Fuse-Knit, or Armo Weft for tailoring.

THREAD
Good-quality polyester, cotton, or silk machine twist.

NEEDLE
70/10 H.

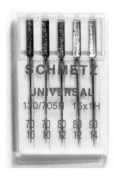

STITCH LENGTH
2.5 mm straight stitch.

PRESSER FOOT
Standard.

SEAM FINISH
Press open and overlock separately, or bind separately with double-fold bias, or Hong Kong finish using lightweight silk as binding. (See #3 on p. 174, #16 on p. 176, #20 on p. 177.) If the garment is lined, press open and overlock separately.

PRESSING
Steam iron on medium-high setting with press cloth.

TOPSTITCHING
Not compatible.

BUTTONHOLES
70/10 H needle with fine machine embroidery thread.

HEM
Finish hem edge with serger, double-fold bias, or Hong Kong finish. Do not use hem depth wider than 1¼ in. or it becomes too heavy. Hand-hem. (See #4 on p. 187, #13 and #15 on p. 189.)

Tip: If interfacing curls during the fusing process, you are probably using an iron with too high heat.

Silk brocade

FABRIC FACT
Since this fabric is crisp, any style requiring drape will make you look heavy.

SUITABLE FOR
Jackets, vests, straight dresses or skirts, narrow pants.

SEWING TIPS
When trimming any seam, trim with pinking shears and no closer than ¼ in. This fabric ravels!

Silk Chiffon

PRESHRINK

Not necessary. Dry-clean completed garment or hand-wash in 1 tablespoon shampoo. Air-dry flat.

LAYOUT

"Without nap" layout, double thickness, using either side of fabric, but be consistent. Mark wrong side of cut pieces.

MARKING

Clo-Chalk or tailor tacks. Do not use waxed chalk because it leaves stains.

CUTTING

To control fabric and cut accurately, cover table with tissue or medical examining paper. Pin double thickness of fabric to paper. Pin pattern through fabric and paper. Keep pins within seam allowances. Using sharp scissors, cut through all layers. Serrated shears are great for this.

INTERFACING

Skin-colored silk organza. Interface top collars and cuffs so that seam allowances won't show through.

THREAD

Fine machine embroidery cotton or silk thread gives best results because it marries with the silk. Polyester thread causes chiffon to pucker.

NEEDLE

60/8 H or 65/9 H, new needle only.

STITCH LENGTH

1.5 mm. to 2.0 mm

PRESSER FOOT

Single-hole throat plate and presser foot. Or use satin stitch foot and switch needle to far left position for support on three sides.

SEAM FINISH

Narrow French seams. On long vertical seams, sew all seams with a tiny zigzag (0.5 mm width and 2.0 mm length). (See #11 on p. 175.)

PRESSING

Dry iron on silk setting. Make sure iron is clean. Steam will cause water spots unless fabric was prewashed.

TOPSTITCHING

Not recommended.

CLOSURES

Machine buttonholes with fine machine embroidery thread or fabric loops. (See #1 on p. 182, #9 on p. 183.) With zippers, interface seam allowances with organza. Put in by hand. (See #5 on p. 180.)

HEM

Options: 1) Thread bobbin with Thread Fuse and use fine thread on top. With wrong side of fabric against the feed dogs, staystitch along hem crease. Trim hem allowance to ½ in. Press to wrong side of fabric. Thread Fuse will dissolve and form sharp crease. Trim hem allowance to ⅛ in. Hand-roll hem and enclose raw edge. Machine-sew with fine thread. Keep finger pressure on back of presser foot to prevent hem from stretching. 2) Hand-roll. Machine-stitch at hem fold with Thread Fuse in bobbin. Trim close to stitching. Hand-roll with damp fingers in a tiny roll and hand-sew with fine machine embroidery thread to reduce bulk. 3) Serged rolled hem. Increase stitch width. Run staystitching line at ½ in. with finger behind presser foot to prevent fabric from stretching. When serging, let rolled hem encase staystitching. Differential feed set at 0.7 helps here. Use fine thread in the serger. (See #16 on p. 189.)

Silk chiffon

FABRIC FACT
Chiffon has a mind of its own.
Do not attempt to work on this
fabric when you are under time
pressure. You and the fabric will
end up in a standoff.

SUITABLE FOR
Full pants, loose tops, and flowing dresses. Look for loose-
fitting simply styled garments
with minimum seams and darts.
Styles that are not full enough
look skimpy. Garments should
be one-third to one-half larger
than your hip measurement and
one-quarter to one-third larger
than your bust measurement. If
your hips are 40 in., full pants
need to measure 53 in. to 60 in.
For a 36-in. bust, the garment
should measure 44 in. to 48 in.

SEWING TIPS
Hold onto top and bobbin
threads when you begin sewing
to prevent fabric from pulling
down into bobbin. Let fabric
feed in naturally.

Silk Dupion

PRESHRINK

Hold steam iron ½ in. above surface. Dry-clean completed garment.

LAYOUT

"With nap" layout, double thickness.

MARKING

Fabric markers, snips in seam allowance, Clo-Chalk.

CUTTING

Rotary cutter or scissors.

INTERFACING

Since this fabric is very prone to wrinkling, I suggest underlining with silk organza. Another alternative is to fuse each garment piece to fusible knitted tricot such as French Fuse or Fuse-Knit. Fusing does flatten the fabric slightly, and the fabric's sheen will show up any place where fusing is not complete. I think the reduction of wrinkles by fusing (70% reduction) is worth the slight change in the fabric. Purists may differ. However, fusing eliminates the fabric's ability to breathe, which if you are constantly warm can be a problem.

THREAD

Good-quality cotton or polyester.

NEEDLE

70/10 H.

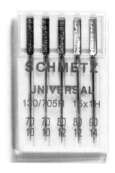

STITCH LENGTH

2.5 mm.

PRESSER FOOT

Standard.

SEAM FINISH

Flat fell, serged and pressed open, bound with Seams Great, or pinked. (See #2 and #3 on p. 174, #9 on p. 175, #19 on p. 176.)

PRESSING

Dry iron on silk setting. Steam will water-spot.

TOPSTITCHING

Close to edge with the help of edge foot or edge-joining foot. (See #3 on p. 180.)

CLOSURES

For buttonholes, use 70/10 HJ needle, fine machine embroidery thread to reduce bulk, and Solvy under presser foot. Loosen top tension slightly. (See #1 on p. 182.)

HEM

Serge or Hong King finish raw edge. Hand-stitch. (See #14 on p. 189.)

Silk dupion

FABRIC FACT
Silk dupion, a crisp fabric with irregular slubs in the yarn, is slightly rougher than Thai silk but not as rough as silk tussah. It is also thicker than Thai silk.

SUITABLE FOR
Narrow or tailored pants, jackets, fitted dresses, straight skirts, or vests.

SEWING TIPS
Easy to sew.

Tip: Did you know that one section of thread moves back and forth through the needle and fabric 60 times before becoming a stitch? All the more reason to use high-quality thread and to change needles frequently.

Silk Georgette

PRESHRINK
Good-quality georgette can be hand-washed in warm water with 1 tablespoon of shampoo. Dry flat. Press lightly with steam. Poor quality loses its crispness. Try a sample before you commit to it.

LAYOUT
"Without nap" layout, double thickness, and glass-head silk pins. Use either side of the fabric, but be consistent. Mark wrong side of cut pieces.

MARKING
Clo-Chalk, tailor tacks, fabric markers. Do not use waxed chalk as it leaves stains.

CUTTING
To control fabric and cut accurately, cover table with tissue or medical examining paper. Pin or staple double thickness of fabric to paper. Pin pattern through fabric and paper. Using sharp scissors, cut through all layers.

INTERFACING
Skin-colored silk organza. Interface top collars and cuffs so that seam allowances won't show through.

THREAD
Fine machine embroidery thread in silk or cotton. Polyester threads cause georgette to pucker.

NEEDLE
New 60/8 H, 65/9 H.

STITCH LENGTH
1.5 mm to 2.0 mm straight stitch.

PRESSER FOOT
Single-hole throat plate or switch presser foot needle to far left position for support on three sides using satin stitch foot.

SEAM FINISH
Narrow French seams. (See #10 on p. 175.)

PRESSING
Dry iron on silk setting. Make sure iron is clean. Steam will cause water spots.

TOPSTITCHING
Not recommended. Hand-pick close to edge. (See #1 on p. 180.)

CLOSURES
Machine buttonholes with fine machine embroidery thread or fabric loops. For zippers, interface the seam allowances with organza. Sew in by hand. (See #5 on p. 180, #1 on p. 182, #9 on p. 183.)

HEM
Options: 1) Thread bobbin with Thread Fuse and fine thread on top. With wrong side of fabric against feed dog, staystitch along hem crease. Trim hem allowance to ½ in. Press to the wrong side of the fabric. Thread Fuse will dissolve and form sharp crease. Trim hem allowance to ⅛ in. Machine-sew with fine thread. Keep finger pressure on back of presser foot to prevent hem from stretching. 2) Hand-roll. Machine-stitch at hem fold with Thread Fuse in bobbin. Trim close to stitching. Hand-roll with dampened fingers in a tiny roll and hand-sew with fine machine embroidery thread to reduce bulk. 3) Serged rolled hem. Run a line of staystitching at ½ in. with finger behind presser foot to prevent fabric from stretching. When serging, let rolled hem encase staystitching. The differential feed set at 0.7 mm helps here. Use a fine serger thread. (See #16 on p. 189.)

Silk georgette

FABRIC FACT

Pebbly weave in georgette gives transparency but slightly more coverage than chiffon. Scarves are often made in this fabric.

SUITABLE FOR

Full pants, loose tops, and flowing dresses. Look for loose-fitting, simply styled garments with a minimum amount of seams and darts. Garments that are not full enough look skimpy. Garments should be one-third to one-half larger than your hip measurement and one-quarter to one-third larger than your bust measurement. If your hips are 40 in., full pants need to measure 53 in. to 60 in. For a 36-in. bust, the garment should measure 45 in. to 48 in.

SEWING TIPS

Hold onto top and bobbin threads when you begin to sew fabric to prevent fabric from pulling into bobbin. Let fabric feed in naturally.

Tip: Prevent frayed and broken threads by using an HE needle when machine-sewing with decorative threads.

Silk Noil

PRESHRINK

Dark colors fade if washed. Preshrink by holding steam iron ½ in. above surface. Dry-clean finished garment. For light colors, machine-wash in warm water and dry on delicate cycle.

LAYOUT

"Without nap" layout.

MARKING

Fabric markers, snips in seam allowances, Clo-Chalk.

CUTTING

Rotary cutter or scissors.

INTERFACING

French Fuse or Fuse-Knit.

THREAD

Good-quality cotton or polyester.

NEEDLE

80/12 H.

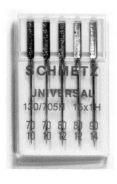

STITCH LENGTH

2.5 mm straight stitch.

PRESSER FOOT

Standard.

SEAM FINISH

Flat fell. (See #9 on p. 175.)

PRESSING

Medium-high heat iron with steam.

TOPSTITCHING

Close to edge with help of edge foot or edge-joining foot. (See #3 on p. 180.)

CLOSURES

For buttonholes, use a 70/10 HJ needle and fine machine embroidery thread to reduce bulk. (See #1 on p. 182.)

HEM

Serge raw edge. Hand-stitch or topstitch with double needle. (See #1 and #4 on p. 187.)

Silk noil

FABRIC FACT
This fabric, sometimes referred to as raw silk, has a dull finish, ravels excessively, and is made from the short waste fibers of silk.

SUITABLE FOR
Full pants, full skirts, big shirts, loose dresses, unstructured loose jackets, and vests if fully interfaced.

SEWING TIPS
Easy to sew.

Tip: If you are not sure of what weight interfacing to use, start with a lighter weight. Heavier weight can always be added.

Silk Organza

PRESHRINK

Hold steam iron ½ in. above surface. Since machine-washing and drying softens organza, wash only if you want to change the hand. Dry-clean finished garment.

LAYOUT

"Without nap" layout, double thickness, using either side of fabric. To be consistent, mark an X on the wrong side of fabric.

MARKING

Clo-Chalk or snips in seam allowance.

CUTTING

Rotary cutter or scissors. Eliminate front facings and substitute second set of fronts to eliminate show-through at edge of facing.

INTERFACING

Self-fabric.

THREAD

Fine cotton machine embroidery or fine silk machine embroidery.

NEEDLE

60/8 H or 65/9 H.

STITCH LENGTH

2.0 mm.

PRESSER FOOT

Use single-hole throat plate and presser foot or switch needle to the far left position for greater fabric support on three sides.

SEAM FINISH

Very narrow French seams. (See #10 on p. 175.)

PRESSING

Make sure iron is very clean of residue. Avoid water spots by using a dry iron on the silk setting.

TOPSTITCHING

Consider shiny rayon thread very close to fabric edge. Use edge foot or edge-joining foot for accuracy. (See #3 on p. 180.)

CLOSURES

For buttonholes, use 70/10 HJ needle and fine machine embroidery thread to reduce bulk or button loops. (See #1 on p. 182, #9 on p. 183.)

HEM

Double roll hem ¼ in. wide, then machine- or hand-stitch. For ruffles, follow these steps:
1. Press a ½-in. fold.
2. Onto the fold align 20-lb. test regular fishing line or 60-lb. test big-game fishing line.
3. Zigzag over fold with monofilament and 2.5 mm wide and 1.5 mm long stitch.
4. Trim fold very close to stitching. 5. Satin stitch edge with 2.5 mm wide and 0.3 mm long stitch. (See #10 on p. 188, #20 on p. 190.)

Silk organza

FABRIC FACT
This fabric adds weight and stands well away from the body.

SUITABLE FOR
Crisp blouses and interfacing. Since this fabric definitely does not drape, choose a style with a very pleasing silhouette that doesn't rely on fabric drape.

SEWING TIPS
Sewing tautly prevents puckered seams. Hold onto top and bottom threads when you begin seam. Don't backstitch—it's too visible.

Tip: Skipped stitches are often caused by a damaged needle, the wrong needle, or the wrong thread. Change each element one at a time to find the culprit.

Silk Shantung

PRESHRINK

Hold steam iron ½ in. above surface. Dry-clean complete garment when necessary. Fabric will lose luster and body if laundered.

LAYOUT

"With nap" layout with slubs going down, double thickness. Because this fabric drapes on the crossgrain, lay out on crossgrain whenever drape is needed.

MARKING

Fabric markers or snips in seam allowance.

CUTTING

Rotary cutter or scissors.

INTERFACING

Since this fabric is prone to wrinkling, I suggest underlining with silk organza. Another alternative is to fuse each garment piece to fusible knitted tricot such as French Fuse or Fuse-Knit. Fusing flattens the fabric slightly, and the shine will show up any place where fusing is not complete. I think the 70% reduction of wrinkles by fusing is worth the slight change in fabric. Purists may differ. However, fusing eliminates the fabric's ability to breathe, which if you are constantly warm can be a problem.

THREAD

Good-quality cotton or polyester.

NEEDLE

70/10 H.

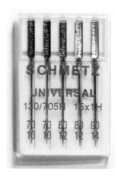

STITCH LENGTH

2.5 mm.

PRESSER FOOT

Standard.

SEAM FINISH

Flat fell, sewn and serged separately, sewn and bound separately with Seams Great, or pinked. (See #2 and #3 on p. 174, #9 on p. 175, #19 on p. 176.)

PRESSING

Dry iron on silk setting. Steam will water-spot.

TOPSTITCHING

Hand-picking or top-stitching ¼ in. from edge. (See #10 on p. 181.)

CLOSURES

For buttonholes, use 70/10 HJ needle, fine machine embroidery thread to reduce bulk, and Solvy under presser foot. Loosen top tension slightly. (See #1 on p. 182.)

HEM

Serge or wrap raw edge with Seams Great. Hand-stitch. (See #4 on p. 187.)

Silk shantung

FABRIC FACT
This fabric's crispness and sheen make it an ideal candidate for a dressy suit.

SUITABLE FOR
Narrow or tailored pants, jackets, fitted dresses, straight skirts, vests, and special-occasion dresses

SEWING TIPS
Easy to sew.

Tip: Funky buttonholes? Make certain you are using the right presser foot. The buttonhole foot has two long grooves on the bottom, which keeps the rows exactly parallel.

Silk Tussah

PRESHRINK

Not necessary. Completed garment must be dry-cleaned.

LAYOUT

"With nap" layout, slubs going down, double thickness. Fabric has some drapability if cut on the crossgrain, making it a good choice for skirts or pants.

MARKING

Fabric markers or snips in seam allowances.

CUTTING

Rotary cutter or scissors.

INTERFACING

Use sew-in interfacing if you don't want to flatten the fabric. Suit Shape, a fusible, flattens the weave very slightly but is still quite attractive and should be used to stabilize the fabric for a jacket or vest. Fuse the entire garment.

THREAD

Good-quality cotton or polyester.

NEEDLE

70/10 H.

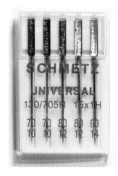

STITCH LENGTH

2.5 mm.

PRESSER FOOT

Standard.

SEAM FINISH

Flat fell, sewn and serged separately, sewn and bound separately with Seams Great, or pinked. (See #2 and #3 on p. 174, #9 on p. 175, and #19 on p. 176.)

PRESSING

Dry iron on silk setting. Steam will water-spot.

TOPSTITCHING

Close to edge or ¼ in. from edge. (See #3 on p. 180, #10 on p. 181.)

CLOSURES

For buttonholes, use 70/10 HJ needle, fine machine embroidery thread to reduce bulk, and Solvy under presser foot. Loosen top tension slightly. (See #1 on p. 182.)

HEM

Turn up 1½-in. hem. Serge or bind raw edge with Seams Great. Hand-stitch. (See #4 on p. 187.)

Silk tussah

FABRIC FACT

Silk tussah is a somewhat rough weave with a nubby appearance. Tussah is not strong and tends to "pill" in areas of wear. Silk tussah is made from uncultivated silk worms; therefore the filaments are course and uneven. Tussah from India is woven from larger threads and is not nearly as refined or drapey as tussah from China.

SUITABLE FOR

Narrow or tailored pants, jackets, straight skirts, vests, and structured garments where little or no drape is required.

SEWING TIPS

Easy to sew.

Tip: If you are new to the world of machine embroidery, put your fabric in a hoop, and loosen the top pressure and the lower feed dog so that the work can be moved around freely.

Silk Tweed

PRESHRINK
Hold steam iron ½ in. above surface. Dry-clean completed garment.

LAYOUT
"Without nap" layout, double thickness.

MARKING
Tailor tacks, fabric markers, Clo-Chalk.

CUTTING
Rotary cutter or scissors. Handle gently to prevent raveling.

INTERFACING
Prevent fabric snags and excess raveling by fusing each garment piece with French Fuse or Fuse-Knit.

THREAD
Good-quality cotton or polyester.

NEEDLE
80/12 H.

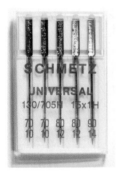

STITCH LENGTH
2.0 mm straight stitch.

PRESSER FOOT
Standard.

SEAM FINISH
Bind seams with double-fold bias or use flat-fell seams. (See #9 on p. 175, #20 on p. 177.)

PRESSING
Steam iron on a silk setting.

TOPSTITCHING
Close to sewn edge with regular thread or ¼ in. from sewn edge with buttonhole twist or shiny rayon thread using an N needle. Edge foot or edge-joining foot helps here. (See #3 on p. 180, #10 on p. 181.)

CLOSURES
For buttonholes, use a 70/10 HJ needle. Cord buttonhole to prevent stretching. Snaps aren't suitable; they will work their way out of the loose weave. (See #5 on p. 182.)

HEM
Finish hem edge with double-fold bias or Hong Kong finish. Hand-hem. (See #15 on p. 189.)

Silk tweed

FABRIC FACT

If you don't have a lot of time to sew, silk tweed is a great choice for a jacket. Choose a tweed that coordinates with the most predominant colors in your wardrobe and you can wear it with everything.

SUITABLE FOR

Jackets and vests, but *not* suitable for straight skirts because it snags too easily or for full pants because it is too bulky.

SEWING TIPS

Easy to sew.

Tip: Silk tweed fabric makes beautiful warm-weather jackets only if the fabric is underlined with fusible knit interfacing. Left to its own devices without interfacing, silk tweed will become baggy in sleeve elbows, pockets, and seat, and is prone to pulled threads.

Slinky Knit

PRESHRINK

Buy an additional ¼ yard per 2-yard length to allow for fabric shrinkage. Hand-wash or machine-wash in warm water on gentle cycle. Machine-dry on cool or dry flat. Do not hang—the fabric will stretch.

LAYOUT

"With nap" layout, double thickness. Support so that fabric does not stretch by hanging off table. Use new pins only in seam allowance or pattern weights.

MARKING

Marking chalk, fabric markers, tailor tacks. No spoke tracing wheels as they will cause snags and runs.

CUTTING

Rotary cutter is the most accurate. For accuracy with scissors, pin double-thickness fabric to tissue paper. Cut fabric and tissue paper at once.

INTERFACING

Textured Weft. Stabilize shoulder, crotch, neckline, and long vertical seams with ¼-in. clear elastic to prevent seam sag.

THREAD

Good-quality polyester.

NEEDLE

75/11 HS.

STITCH LENGTH

3.0 mm.

PRESSER FOOT

Walking foot. Reduce pressure on presser foot. Loosen top tension slightly.

SEAM FINISH

Sew seams with 3-thread serger, with woolly nylon on both loopers. Use differential feed if you have it. If garment is close-fitting, sew seam initially with small zigzag, then serge seams together with 3-thread serger right next to it. (See #21 and #23 on p. 177.)

PRESSING

Medium-temperature iron with lots of steam. Press seams open on seam stick to prevent seam imprint on the outside.

TOPSTITCHING

Not successful because of fabric stretch. Consider substituting hand-picking close to the edge. (See #1 on p. 180.)

CLOSURES

Invisible zippers work well here. Consider other buttonhole alternatives such as button loops and snaps. Because this fabric is heavy, stronger elastic is needed for elasticized waists. Handler Non-roll Monofilament elastic works well. (See #9 on p. 183, #11 on p. 184.)

HEM

Stabilize hem allowance with fusible interfacing serged on the raw edge with glue side out so that when hem is pressed it fuses lightly to garment. This technique prevents hem from stretching as it is machine hemmed. Use Teflon or walking foot for double-needle topstitching. Use double-needle ZWI stretch with hand-wrapped woolly nylon on bobbin. Bypass guide in bobbin case and loosen upper tension slightly. (See #1 on p. 187.)

Slinky knit

FABRIC FACT

This fabric drapes extremely well and never wrinkles, making it great for traveling. There are different grades of slinky knit. The heavier weight gives the best performance and shrinks the least. This acetate fabric snags easily. Make sure nails and cuticles are smooth and hands free of lotions, which will transfer grease spots to the fabric.

SUITABLE FOR

Simple styling and few pattern pieces: wrap styles, A-line or gored skirts, and full dresses. Fabric has wonderful drape but needs to be at least 4 in. bigger than the body or it looks skimpy and too figure revealing. Between 4 in. and 10 in. of ease is recommended.

SEWING TIPS

Use pins in seam allowances only. To start seam, start sewing for 1 in. on Solvy positioned between feed dog and fabric. Hold onto threads when you begin. As an alternative to facings, trim neckline seam allowance to ⅜ in. Serge ¼-in.-wide clear elastic to the wrong side of neckline raw edge. Turn under ⅜ in. Topstitch with a double-needle ZWI stretch 4.0 mm width from the right side. Prevent darts from stretching as you sew by sewing through ¼-in. twill tape or selvage cut to size from the pattern.

Tip: Every wardrobe could use a pair of black trousers in 3- or 4-ply silk for trans-seasonal use. Perfect a good pants pattern and stick with it.

Suede

PRESHRINK

Not necessary. Store rolled up or perfectly flat. Do not wrap in plastic. To care for suede, spot-clean with cornmeal or suede cleaner. Avoid dry cleaning for as long as possible since dry cleaning dries out the natural tannins. Suede is never as supple after dry cleaning.

LAYOUT

The grainline runs along the backbone of the skin. Suede has a nap. Lay pieces in direction of nap from neck to tail. Mark nap on back of skin. Examine skins for flaws and circle on the wrong side. Place skin wrong side up, single thickness. Make extra pattern pieces so that you have a left and right piece for economical cutting. Use pattern weights.

MARKING

Fabric markers or pencils. No waxed-based marking chalk as it leaves stains.

CUTTING

Rotary cutter or scissors.

INTERFACING

Sew-in or low-temperature fusible such as Touch o' Gold or Soft 'n' Silky.

THREAD

Polyester only. Tannins will rot cotton thread.

NEEDLE

70/10 HJ for light-weight skins, 90/14 NTW for pig suede, and glover's needle for hand-sewing.

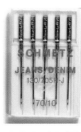

STITCH LENGTH

3.0 mm.

PRESSER FOOT

Walking foot or roller foot.

SEAM FINISH

Sew plain seam. Seam finish with fake flat fell. Press seam open, then trim one seam allowance. Flip other seam allowance over trimmed one. Topstitch into place from right side ¼ in. from seam. (See #27 on p. 178.)

PRESSING

Medium heat dry iron. Use press-and-lift motion to avoid stretching the skin. Use brown bag for a press cloth on the right side.

TOPSTITCHING

On details, stitch very close to edge. Edge foot or edge-joining foot helps here. (See #3 on p. 180.)

CLOSURES

Bound buttonholes, snaps, button loops, or eyelets and lacing. (See #9 on p. 183, #11 on p. 184, #15 on p. 185.)

HEM

Double row of topstitching on thin suede. Barge rubber cement on heavier suede. (See #7 on p. 188, #23 on p. 190.)

Suede

FABRIC FACT
Suede can be lamb suede, pig suede, deer skin, or chamois. Suede is sold by the square foot, not by the yard. To calculate how much yardage to buy, multiply the yardage needed for 45-in.-wide fabric by 11.25, then multiply again by 1.25. This will give you the amount in square feet. For example, if 3 yards of 45-in.-wide fabric is needed, then 3 x 11.25 = 33.75 x 1.25 = 42.48 or 42½ square feet. Make sure all hides come from the same dye lot.

SUITABLE FOR
If skins are very soft and drapey like lamb suede, use for loose shirts, jackets, semi-fitted pants, or loose pants. Pig suede is less drapey and needs a more fitted skirt or pants. Pretest pattern because stitches leave permanent holes. Suede in any grain makes nice trim on woolen or tapestry fabrics.

SEWING TIPS
Use paper clips to hold seams together, and pin only at seam joints. Do not backstitch, which weakens the fabric. Hold onto top and bobbin threads when you start sewing.

Sueded Rayon

PRESHRINK

Machine-wash in cool water on delicate cycle; machine-dry on low temperature.

MARKING

Fabric markers or snips in the seam allowance.

CUTTING

Rotary cutter or scissors. Use cut-on facings whenever possible.

INTERFACING

Interfacing is rarely necessary since fabric has so much natural body. Use self-fabric only for interfacing since rayon stretches and will bag over any other interfacing.

THREAD

Good-quality cotton or polyester.

NEEDLE

70/10 HJ or 70/10 HM.

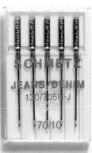

STITCH LENGTH

Tiny zigzag (0.5 mm width, 2.5 mm length). This will allow seam to relax as fabric relaxes.

PRESSER FOOT

Standard presser foot with needle in far left position.

SEAM FINISH

Press open and serge or flat fell. (See #3 on p. 174, #9 on p. 175.)

PRESSING

Dry iron on medium-high setting.

TOPSTITCHING

Very close to finished edge with the help of edge foot or edge-joining foot. (See #3 on p. 180.)

CLOSURES

For buttonholes, use 70/10 HJ needle and fine machine embroidery thread to reduce bulk. Snaps can also work. Interface behind snaps with a 1-in. circle of firm interfacing. (See #1 on p. 182, #11 on p. 184.)

HEM

Serge hem edge and hand-stitch. (See #4 on p. 187.)

Sueded rayon

Tip: When eliminating a waistband with facing or lining, don't forget to use stay-tape on the waistline seam to prevent stretching during wearing.

FABRIC FACT
While this fabric is washable, it does become more compact, making it slightly thicker. Sueded fabric does not drape as well as sandwashed silk.

SUITABLE FOR
Full pants, full skirts, loose unstructured tops, and full shorts.

SEWING TIPS
Sew tautly, pulling with equal pressure from front and back as you sew.

Sweatshirting

PRESHRINK

Buy an additional ¼ yard for every 2 yards purchased. Sew crosswise ends together to prevent stretching during washing. Fabric has progressive shrinkage, which means it must be machine-washed in warm water and dried at regular temperature two times before cutting out. Wash separately—this fabric produces a lot of lint.

LAYOUT

"Without nap" layout, double thickness. Use pattern weights—pins tear tissue. If crosswise ends won't lie flat, use spray starch and an iron to flatten.

MARKING

Snips at notches, tailor's chalk, fabric markers.

CUTTING

Rotary cutter or scissors.

INTERFACING

French Fuse or Fuse-Knit.

THREAD

Polyester is the best choice since it has some stretch. Wind bobbin slowly.

NEEDLE

75/11 HS.

STITCH LENGTH

Tiny zigzag (0.5 mm width, 3.0 mm length).

PRESSER FOOT

Teflon or walking foot.

SEAM FINISH

Sew seams first with a tiny zigzag. Reduce pressure on presser foot or keep finger pushing fabric behind presser foot to prevent stretching. Use triple stitch on your conventional machine to stitch areas of stress such as crotch and underarm seams. Finish seams with a 3- or 4-thread overlock with woolly nylon on loopers. (See #21 on p. 177.) Use differential feed or your finger behind presser foot to prevent stretching as you serge.

PRESSING

Steam iron on cotton setting.

TOPSTITCHING

¼ in. from finished edge using edge foot or edge-joining foot as a guide, lengthening stitch to 4.0 mm. (See #10 on p. 181.)

CLOSURES

Stabilize buttonhole area with lengthwise grain parallel to buttonhole. For buttonholes, use 70/10 HJ using Solvy between the presser foot and sweatshirt fabric. Cord buttonholes to prevent stretching. Stabilize zipper seam allowances with ½-in. strips of fusible interfacing. (See #5 on p. 182, #18 on p. 176.)

HEM

Ribbing, or serge raw edge. Topstitch with double-needle ZWI stretch using woolly nylon in both loopers. (See #17 on p. 189.)

Sweatshirting

FABRIC FACT
Some grades of sweat-shirt fabric are thicker and more colorfast than others. Buy ¼ yard and run it through the laundry, then decide whether it is worth your time to construct a garment from it.

SUITABLE FOR
Sweatshirts and jogging suits.

SEWING TIPS
Stabilize neck, shoulders, and waistline seams with ¼-in. clear elastic.

Tip: Prevent buttonholes on knits, loose wovens, or jackets from stretching by cording the buttonhole.

Taffeta

PRESHRINK

Not necessary. Dry-clean complete garment. Machine-washing and machine-drying create an interesting, pebbly appearance that can hide puckered seams.

LAYOUT

"With nap" layout, double thickness.

MARKING

Clips in seam allowance. No waxed chalk as it leaves spots.

CUTTING

Rotary cutter or scissors.

INTERFACING

Durapress sew-in.

THREAD

Good-quality polyester or cotton.

NEEDLE

70/10 HJ.

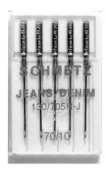

STITCH LENGTH

2.5 mm straight stitch.

PRESSER FOOT

Standard.

SEAM FINISH

Serge all edges before seaming since fabric ravels excessively. Seam and press open. (See #3 on p. 174.)

PRESSING

Steam iron on medium setting. Always use an organza press cloth to prevent water spots. If taffeta has been washed for a pebbly texture, water-spotting is not a problem. Press over a rounded seam stick or use brown bag strips under seam allowances to prevent seam show-through.

TOPSTITCHING

Rarely appropriate.

CLOSURES

For buttonholes use 70/10 HJ needle. (See #1 on p. 182.)

HEM

¼-in. double-roll machine hem or rolled hem on the serger. (See #10 on p. 188, #16 on p. 189.)

Taffeta

FABRIC FACT

Taffeta is a noisy fabric that rustles when you walk. Taffeta also creases easily, which can be reduced by under-lining in organza or net. Fabric does not ease well, so choose a style without princess seams.

SUITABLE FOR

Full skirts and party dresses.

SEWING TIPS

Experiment with tension on scrap fabric. Puckers become permanent. Sew tautly, pulling with equal pressure from front and back.

Tip: On any fabric that must be matched, like a print or plaid, the top fabric can shift while sewing despite your best efforts at matching the pattern. Use a walking foot and feed both layers into the needle at the same time.

Tencel

PRESHRINK

Machine-wash on regular cycle in warm water. Machine-dry on permanent press. Remove fabric promptly from dryer to prevent wrinkles from setting. Completed garment can be washed or dry-cleaned.

LAYOUT

"Without nap" layout, double thickness.

MARKING

Fabric markers or tracing wheel.

CUTTING

Rotary cutter or scissors.

INTERFACING

Sofbrush, Sof Shape, Fuse-Knit, and French Fuse.

THREAD

Cotton gives best results.

NEEDLE

70/10 HM, 70/10 HJ, 70/10 H.

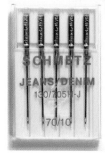

STITCH LENGTH

2.5 mm straight stitch.

PRESSER FOOT

Standard.

SEAM FINISH

Flat fell or serge separately and press open. (See #3 on p. 174, #9 on p. 175.)

PRESSING

Steam iron at medium temperature.

TOPSTITCHING

Close to the finished edge, with the help of edge foot or edge-joining foot or ¼ in. away from finished edge. Lengthen stitch to 3.5 mm. (See #3 on p. 180.)

CLOSURES

For buttonholes use 70/10 HJ needle. (See #1 on p. 182.)

HEM

Serge raw hem edge. Topstitch with double needle or glue up with ultralight Stitch Witchery. (See #1 and #3 on p. 187.)

Tencel

FABRIC FACT

Tencel is a fabric made from wood pulp and produced with a recyclable non-toxic dissolving agent. Tencel is soft and drapey and often combined with other fibers in both knits and wovens. It is comfortable to wear, behaving very much like cotton without as much wrinkling. It does wrinkle however, and does not make a great travel garment.

SUITABLE FOR

Styles that need to be soft and drapey such as full pants, fullish skirts, big shirts, and pajamas.

SEWING TIPS

Easy to sew.

Tip: Simple styling and plain fabric make an ideal canvas for beautiful buttons.

Terrycloth

PRESHRINK

Buy an additional ¼ yard for every 2 yards cut. Fabric has progressive shrinkage, which means it must be machine-washed in warm water and dried at regular temperature twice before cutting out.

LAYOUT

"Without nap" layout, double layer. Pattern weights are better for holding pattern to the fabric since pins will tear the tissue.

MARKING

Fabric markers, adhesive dots, or safety pins.

CUTTING

Rotary cutter or scissors. Serge all edges immediately to prevent raveling. A 4-thread serger stitch adheres to fabric more securely than a 3-thread serger and will not pull off.

INTERFACING

None. Fabric has enough body on its own.

THREAD

Good-quality cotton or polyester.

NEEDLE

80/12 H or 90/12 H.

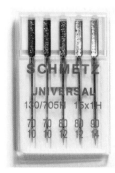

STITCH LENGTH

3.0 mm.

PRESSER FOOT

Teflon.

SEAM FINISH

For the least bulk, sew seam with straight stitch (3.0 mm). Press open. Topstitch seam allowance on each side to the garment with 3-step zigzag. Stitching is not visible because it sinks into the terry-cloth. (See #31 on p. 178.)

PRESSING

Steam iron on cotton setting.

TOPSTITCHING

¼ in. from finished edge with double needle. (See #1 on p. 187.)

CLOSURES

Stabilize buttonhole area with lengthwise grain parallel to buttonhole. For buttonholes, use 70/10 HJ using Solvy between the presser foot and the terry. Cord buttonhole to prevent stretching. Snaps are a good alternative but must be well interfaced between layers or snaps will peel away from fabric. Zippers are not recommended—too bulky. (See #5 on p. 182, #11 on p. 184.)

HEM

Flat lock or serge raw edge. Turn up 1¼ in. Topstitch with double needle and lengthen stitch to 4.0 mm. (See #2 on p. 187.)

Tip: Velour and stretch terry have progressive shrinkage, which means they continue to shrink after the first wash-and-dry process. Purchase shrink insurance by buying an additional ¼ yard of fabric. Machine-wash and machine-dry twice before cutting.

Terrycloth

FABRIC FACT
Terrycloth is 100% cotton, absorbent, and comfortable to wear. Expensive terrycloth robes are advertised as French terry. This is terrycloth with a small percentage of Lycra.

SUITABLE FOR
Beach jackets and robes.

SEWING TIPS
Stabilize neck, shoulders, and waistline seams with ¼-in. clear elastic. Eliminate facings whenever possible. Options: 1) Staystitch then clip curves. Overlock raw edge. Turn under using staystitching line to help you. Topstitch with double needle or flatlock. 2) Bind edges with double-fold bias or cotton knit strips cut on the crossgrain.

Tulle & Net

PRESHRINK

Not necessary.

LAYOUT

"Without nap" layout, double thickness.

MARKING

Safety pins or tailor tacks made with yarn.

CUTTING

Rotary cutter or scissors.

INTERFACING

Self-fabric.

THREAD

Good-quality polyester or cotton.

NEEDLE

70/10 H.

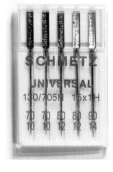

STITCH LENGTH

1.5 mm straight stitch.

PRESSER FOOT

Standard.

SEAM FINISH

French seams. (See #10 on p. 175.)

PRESSING

Low-temperature dry iron.

TOPSTITCHING

Not necessary.

CLOSURES

Buttonholes are not rec-
ommended because
they will pull out of the
fabric. Substitute but-
ton loops or very small
snaps. (See #9 on
p. 183, #11 on p. 184.)

HEM

Options: 1) Not neces-
sary since fabric doesn't
ravel. 2) Use rayon em-
broidery thread to
zigzag over rat-tail cord
½ in. from edge. Trim
off excess later. 3) Use
grooved presser foot to
zigzag over topstitching
thread. Pull slightly on
fabric behind the foot.
4) Serge or zigzag over
25-lb. fishing line for a
flounced effect. (See
#20 and #22 on
p. 190.)

Tulle & net

FABRIC FACT
Since so few people sew bridal or dressy dresses, color selection in tulle and net is extremely limited unless you go to one of the larger, well-established mail-order houses. Consider purchasing white and dying it to the color you want.

SUITABLE FOR
Interfacing behind lace, bridal veils, underskirts with multiple layers, sleeve heads, underlining in satins and taffetas, and slightly transparent portions of a bodice.

SEWING TIPS
Easy to sew.

Tip: If tailor tacks are the only markings visible on your fabric, use different-color threads for different markings. For example, use one color for darts, another color for pleats, and another color for buttonholes.

Upholstery

PRESHRINK

Fabric is too stiff to use "as is" for garments. Overlock crossgrain ends to prevent unraveling. Machine-wash in warm water. Machine-dry on regular cycle. Some upholstery fabrics appear more muted after machine-washing.

LAYOUT

"Without nap" layout, double thickness. Use pattern weights. Eliminate as many seams as possible to take advantage of fabric design.

MARKING

Chalk or tailor tacks.

CUTTING

Sharp scissors or rotary cutter.

INTERFACING

Armo Weft.

THREAD

Good-quality cotton or polyester.

NEEDLE

90/14 HJ or 100/16 HJ.

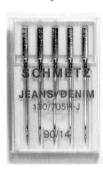

STITCH LENGTH

3.0 mm straight stitch.

PRESSER FOOT

Walking foot works best for high-texture upholstery or if pattern matching is necessary.

SEAM FINISH

Press seams open. Bind with double-fold bias. (See #20 on p. 177.)

PRESSING

Cotton setting with steam. Pound seams flat with a tailor's clapper.

TOPSTITCHING

¼ in. from edge, lengthening stitch to 4.0 mm. Use topstitching thread and an N needle. (See #10 on p. 181.)

CLOSURES

Since this fabric ravels so easily, consider alternatives to buttonholes, such as button loops or frogs. (See #9 on p. 183, #12 on p. 184.)

HEM

Finish raw edge with double-fold bias. Hand-hem. (See #15 on p. 189.) If garment is unlined, consider using faux leather to finish all edges, eliminating hems altogether. (See #9 on p. 188.)

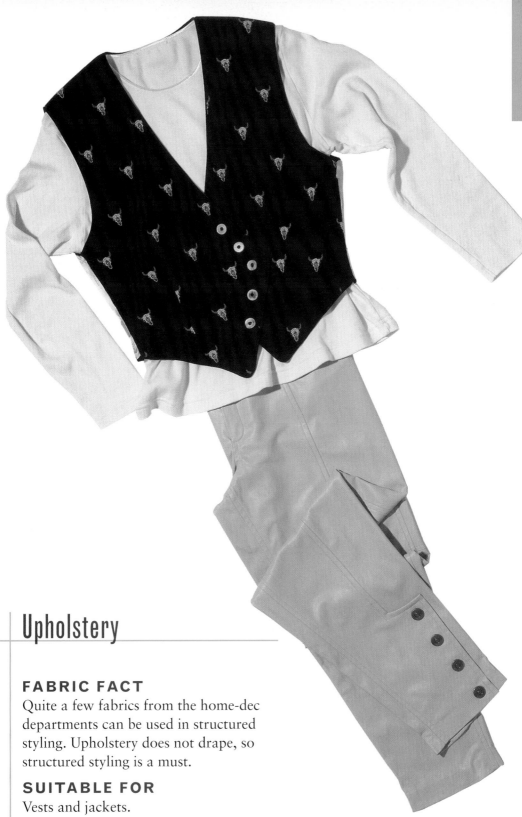

Upholstery

FABRIC FACT
Quite a few fabrics from the home-dec departments can be used in structured styling. Upholstery does not drape, so structured styling is a must.

SUITABLE FOR
Vests and jackets.

SEWING TIPS
Because of upholstery's tendency to ravel, serge all edges immediately after cutting. On a conventional machine, sew tautly, pulling with equal pressure from front and back as you sew.

Velour

PRESHRINK
Buy an additional ¼ yard for every 2 yards cut. Fabric has progressive shrinkage, which means it must be machine-washed in warm water and dried at regular temperature two times before cutting out.

LAYOUT
"With nap" layout, double thickness and wrong sides together or single layer if fabric is thick. Use pattern weights.

MARKING
Clips in seam allowance, Clo-Chalk, tailor tacks.

CUTTING
Rotary cutter or scissors. Cut wider seam allowances to overcome curling edges. Excess can be trimmed off as you serge.

INTERFACING
Fuse-Knit or French Fuse.

THREAD
Good-quality cotton or polyester.

NEEDLE
75/11 HS.

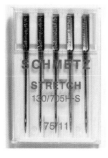

STITCH LENGTH
Small zigzag (0.5 mm width, 3.0 mm length).

PRESSER FOOT
Walking foot.

SEAM FINISH
Sew seams first with a tiny zigzag. Serge seams together with woolly nylon on both loopers. (See #21 on p. 177.)

PRESSING
Place right side of fabric against needle board or fluffy towel. Use steam iron on a cotton setting on wrong side only.

TOPSTITCHING
Close to the edge with the help of edge foot or edge-joining foot. Lengthen stitch to 3.5 mm. (See #3 on p. 180.)

CLOSURES
Stabilize buttonhole area with lengthwise grain parallel to buttonhole. Use 70/10 HJ and fine thread, using Solvy between the presser foot and the knit. Sew a corded buttonhole to prevent stretching. Stabilize zipper seam allowances with 1-in. strips of fusible interfacing cut with pinking shears. Invisible zippers preferred. (See #18 on p. 176, #5 on p. 182.)

HEM
Options: 1) Fuse with ½-in. strip of Stitch Witchery ultralight fusible web. Then sew with double-needle ZWI stretch with woolly nylon hand-wrapped on the bobbin and a Teflon presser foot. 2) Use a stretch blindstitch, using woolly nylon hand-wrapped on the bobbin and regular thread on top. 3) Flatlock. 4) Ribbing. (See #1, #2, and #6 on p. 187, #17 on p. 189.)

Velour

FABRIC FACT

Grades of velour vary. Look for the thicker variety, which keeps its shape, drapes better, and has more depth of color. Many of the newer velours have Lycra content, making them drape better.

SUITABLE FOR

Robes, loose tops, overshirts, caftans.

SEWING TIPS

Do not stretch fabric as you sew. Push into presser foot. Reduce pressure on presser foot or keep finger pushing fabric behind presser foot to prevent stretching whether sewing on a conventional machine or a serger.

Tip: Always hang velour fabric for 24 hours after preshrinking. A heavy velour can stretch 6 in. in length.

Vinyl

PRESHRINK
Not necessary.

LAYOUT
Single thickness. Grainline is not important—pattern pieces may be positioned in any direction for fabric economy. Use pattern weights. Needle holes are permanent.

MARKING
Adhesive dots or colored pencils on the wrong side. No spoked tracing wheel as it leaves holes.

CUTTING
Heavy-duty shears or large rotary cutter for thick vinyl.

INTERFACING
Sew-in such as Durapress.

THREAD
Good-quality polyester or cotton on thin weights, upholstery thread on thicker weights.

NEEDLE
70/10 HJ or 70/10 H for thin weights, 140/16 HJ for thicker weights.

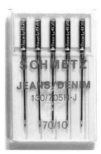

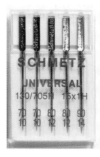

STITCH LENGTH
Use a longer stitch (3.5 mm); smaller stitches will weaken fabric.

PRESSER FOOT
Teflon or roller foot. Loosen top tension slightly.

SEAM FINISH
No overlocking as it stretches seam. Options: 1) Mock flat-fell seam. (See #27 on p. 178.) 2) Finger-press open and glue.

PRESSING
Test scrap. Some vinyl melts even under a very low-temperature iron and must be finger-pressed open only. Others tolerate low-temperature iron. A press cloth must be used.

TOPSTITCHING
For lightweight vinyl, topstitching is not recommended. Topstitching devalues the finished garment. On heavier-weight vinyl, topstitching can be quite attractive ¼ in. from finished edge. Use an N needle and 4.0 mm length stitch or polyester topstitch thread.

CLOSURES
Snaps using interfacing between layers. (See #11 on p. 184.) YKK zippers on coats and jackets, invisible zippers on skirts and pants.

HEM
Turn up a 2-in. hem. Binding raw hem edge with Seams Great is very important to prevent lightweight vinyl from running like hosiery. Glue up hem with fabric glue or turn under ½ in. and topstitch. (See #7 on p. 188.)

Vinyl

FABRIC FACT

Vinyl shines like patent leather, does not breathe, and is fun to wear. Garments are much more comfortable and wrinkle less if they are lined.

SUITABLE FOR

Upholstery projects, handbags, straight skirts, narrow pants, vests, and jean jacket trim. Avoid curved seams as in princess styles. Layers of vinyl stick together, making it very difficult to sew two reverse curves together.

SEWING TIPS

Spray machine surface with silicone spray to avoid sticking if sewing on the right side. If you still have problems, resort to strips of tissue paper between the presser foot and the fabric and the fabric and the feed dogs. Cut a space for feed dogs out of Teflon press sheet. Tape to sewing table surface and fabric will slide easily. Needle holes are permanent. Hold layers together with paper clips.

Waterproof, Non-Breathables

PRESHRINK

Not necessary. Machine-wash in cold water. Rinse two times to prevent the soap from clogging fabric pores. Machine-dry on low heat.

LAYOUT

"Without nap" layout, double thickness. Fabrics are coated, so they can be cut lengthwise or crosswise because the coating stabilizes them.

MARKING

Chalk or smooth tracing wheel.

CUTTING

Rotary cutter or scissors.

INTERFACING

No fusibles; sew-in such as Durapress.

THREAD

Good-quality polyester for lightweight fabrics; nylon for heavyweight in areas of high stress.

NEEDLE

70/10 HM or 70/10 H for lighter weight; 80/12 H, 80/12 HM, 90/14 HM, 90/14 H for heavier weights.

STITCH LENGTH

2.5 mm straight stitch.

PRESSER FOOT

Teflon or walking foot.

SEAM FINISH

On coated fabrics, press seams open or to one side, and iron on strips of seam sealant or seam-sealant glue. For second option, trim one seam allowance and flip the other one over on top of it. Topstitch ¼ in. from seamline on right side. Seal all seams with seam-sealant tape or seam-sealant glue unless you don't plan to wear in extreme weather conditions. (See #33 and #34 on p. 179.)

PRESSING

Press lightly with a low-temperature, dry iron. Experiment on a scrap to see if fabric melts or sticks to the iron. If not, go ahead and press.

TOPSTITCHING

¼ in. away from finished edge. (See #10 on p. 181.)

CLOSURES

YKK plastic zippers, snaps, Velcro, or the softer hook-and-loop closures called Fixvelour. (See #11 on p. 184, #16 on p. 185, #19 on p. 186.)

HEM

Ribbing is not recommended since it traps water. Since the fabric is rather stiff, use narrow (¾-in.) plain hems, casings with elastic or drawstrings in drawstring shock cord, or faux leather or vinyl binding as seen here. (See #31 on p. 192.)

Waterproof, non-breathables

FABRIC FACT
These non-slippery fabrics are sold under the names Glacier, Oxford, Cordura, Sportlight, Linebacker, and Quarterback. Fabric surface is coated on the outside with a polyurethane or polyvinyl chloride (PVC) coating, making it impervious to water. These fabrics, while they are truly waterproof, do not breathe. The cost for these fabrics is considerably less than for waterproof breathables.

SUITABLE FOR
Soft luggage and bags, ponchos, ski jackets, rain suits. Avoid patch pockets, which trap water.

SEWING TIPS
Install eyelets in underarm area to allow for air circulation. Use absorbent lining such as Hydrofil or Coolmax to reduce the clammy feeling when wet.

Wetsuit

PRESHRINK

Not necessary. For completed garments, machine-wash in warm water. Air-dry or machine-dry on low temperature.

LAYOUT

"Without nap" layout, single layer.

MARKING

Chalk or snips in the seam allowance.

CUTTING

Large rotary cutter or scissors.

INTERFACING

Not necessary.

THREAD

Nylon.

NEEDLE

75/11 HS.

STITCH LENGTH

Tiny zigzag (0.5 mm width, 2.5 mm length).

PRESSER FOOT

Standard.

SEAM FINISH

Serging the seams with a flatlock stitch is your best choice since bulk is eliminated on the inside. Second choice would be to sew with a small zigzag (0.5 mm width, 2.5 mm length) and serge seams closed with a 4-thread serger using woolly nylon on both loopers. (See #9 on p. 175, #21 on p. 177.)

PRESSING

None.

TOPSTITCHING

Flatlock ¼ in. from edge. (See #6 on p. 181.)

CLOSURES

YKK plastic zippers. (See #19 on p. 186.)

HEM

Turn up ¾-in. hem. Machine-stitch with triple zigzag for the most stretch. Flatlock on the serger is also suitable. (See #6 on p. 181, #27 on p. 191.)

Wetsuit

FABRIC FACT

Sold under the brand names Neoprene and Polartec Thermal Stretch, wetsuit fabrics are designed to keep you warm, even when wet. Neoprene has a foam layer between Lycra layers. Polartec Thermal Stretch has a polyester fleece layer between Lycra layers.

SUITABLE FOR

Wetsuits and any water sportswear.

SEWING TIPS

Easy to sew.

Tip: A roller foot is the answer to sewing on foam-backed fabrics.

Wool Boucle

PRESHRINK
Hold steam iron ½ in. above fabric surface.

LAYOUT
"With nap" layout, single thickness. Use pattern weights.

MARKING
Tailor tacks.

CUTTING
Rotary cutter or sharp scissors.

INTERFACING
Sew-in interfacing like Durapress to avoid flattening texture.

THREAD
Good-quality silk, polyester, or cotton.

NEEDLE
80/12 H.

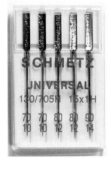

STITCH LENGTH
3.0 mm straight stitch.

PRESSER FOOT
Walking or roller foot.

SEAM FINISH
Straight seam. Serge seams together and press to one side. (See #4 on p. 174.)

PRESSING
Steam iron on wool setting. Use press cloth on right side. Be careful not to overpress or you will flatten the texture. Do not use a clapper on this fabric. Flatten finished edges with hand-picking since overpressing will flatten surface.

TOPSTITCHING
Hand-picking ⅛ in. from finished edge.

CLOSURES
Corded machine buttonhole or faced buttonhole. (See #1 on p. 182, #6 on p. 183.)

HEM
Hand-hem. Stretch hem every 4 in. and knot. (See #4 on p. 187.)

Tip: Prevent knit seams from stretching and curling by placing your finger behind the presser foot on the overlock machine.

Wool boucle

FABRIC FACT
Boucle is a loosely woven or knitted fabric with small curls or loops that provide a nubby surface.

SUITABLE FOR
Sweater looks, vest, unstructured coats.

SEWING TIPS
Push fabric into the presser foot.

Wool Crepe

PRESHRINK

Must be preshrunk at dry cleaner or the garment will shrink a whole size the first time it is dry-cleaned. If you did not preshrink fabric at the dry cleaner, ask for low-heat steam pressing when dry cleaning and shrinkage will be greatly minimized.

LAYOUT

"Without nap" layout, double thickness.

MARKING

Clo-Chalk or tailor tacks.

CUTTING

Rotary cutter or scissors. Cutting seam allowance ¼ in. wider will enable seams to press flatter.

INTERFACING

Textured Weft or Armo Weft. Underline jackets with cotton batiste for best results in jackets.

THREAD

Good-quality cotton, polyester, or silk.

NEEDLE

80/12 H.

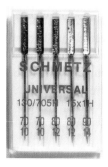

STITCH LENGTH

2.5 mm.

PRESSER FOOT

Standard.

SEAM FINISH

Options: 1) Overlock seam allowances separately with woolly nylon on the lower looper. 2) If lined, no seam finish is necessary. (See #3 on p. 174.)

PRESSING

With a steam iron on the wool setting, press seams as stitched. Press seams open over a seam stick or half-round to prevent seam shadows. On the right side, use a self-fabric press cloth and press again.

TOPSTITCHING

Topstitch by machine ¼ in. from finished edge or hand-pick with shiny rayon or pearl cotton thread. (See #1 on p. 180, #10 on p. 181.)

CLOSURES

Use cord to prevent machine buttonholes from stretching, or use bound buttonholes. (See #5 on p. 182, #8 on p. 183.)

HEM

Serge or Hong Kong finish raw edge. Turn up 1½ in. Hand-sew. (See #4 on p. 187, #13 on p. 189.)

Wool crepe

FABRIC FACT
Crepe is a twisted weave fabric with a pebbly appearance that doesn't wrinkle. While wool crepe is the most common, silk, rayon, and very occasionally cotton crepes are also available. Wool crepe varies in quality. More expensive wool crepe resists wrinkles better and is more opaque than its less expensive look-alikes.

SUITABLE FOR
Tailored pants, straight skirts, jackets, full skirts on bias, or semi-fitted dresses. Since this fabric is stable but does drape, it is very flattering on the body.

SEWING TIPS
Very easy to sew. Stay-tape all areas of stress.

Tip: Applying fusible interfacing onto wool crepe is not recommended because it changes the hand of this beautiful, soft fabric. I suggest underlining the entire jacket with a soft lightweight fabric such as cotton batiste, pima cotton, or voile. Underlining will conceal hand stitches in the hem as well as provide a base for fusible interfacing.

Wool Double Cloth

PRESHRINK
Hold steam iron ½ in. above surface.

LAYOUT
"With nap" layout, single thickness. Use pattern weights.

MARKING
Tailor tacks or tailor's chalk.

CUTTING
Scissors or rotary cutter.

INTERFACING
None—fabric has enough body on its own.

THREAD
Silk, since it marries with the fabric.

NEEDLE
90/14 H.

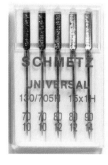

STITCH LENGTH
3.0 mm to 3.5 mm.

PRESSER FOOT
Teflon.

SEAM FINISH
Options: 1) Butt edges together over 1½-in.-wide wool jersey strip. Machine-sew a featherstitch. This joins the layers while attaching to the strip. Trim down one side of the wool strip, and wrap the other around and hand-stitch. Sew darts in the same manner, cutting out bulk in darts. (See #14 on p. 176.) This method is my favorite because it eliminates bulk. 2) The following method is much more time-consuming and for those who like handwork. To make seam construction invisible, pull apart layers 1¼ in. in seam area. Sew a ⅝-in. seam in outer layer. Press open. On inner layers, trim seam to ⅜ in. Fold in ¼ in. to ⅜ in. until folds meet. Press. Slipstitch inner seam allowances together. (See #30 on p. 178.)

PRESSING
Use steam iron on wool setting. Use piece of wool as a press cloth when pressing on right side.

TOPSTITCHING
Hand-picking ⅜ in. from edge, if desired. (See #1 on p. 180.)

CLOSURES
Corded buttonholes. (See #5 on p. 182.) Consider button loops as a substitute for buttonholes or faced buttonhole openings. (See #6 and #9 on p. 183.)

HEM
Bind edge with crossgrain wool jersey or faux leather. For the hand-sewing enthusiast, separate layers 1¼ in. Miter corners separately on both layers. Turn in edges ⅝ in. Trim under layer seam allowance to ⅜ in. Slipstitch layers together. (See #9 on p. 188, #26 on p. 191.)

Tip: A large coat
in double cloth
can make you
look big if you
lean in that
direction.

Wool double cloth

FABRIC FACT
Wool double cloth is actually two
different fabrics joined with threads
in between that are invisible from
either side of the fabric. Wool double cloth is terrific if you want to
make a reversible garment.

SUITABLE FOR
Because this fabric is bulky, choose
a shape that does not rely on drape
for coats and vests.

SEWING TIPS
Easy to sew.

Woolens & Worsteds

PRESHRINK

Hold steam iron ½ in. above surface or preshrink at the dry cleaner.

LAYOUT

"With nap" layout with woolens (not always mandatory but a good safeguard); "without nap" layout for worsteds, double thickness.

MARKING

Tailor tacks or tailor's chalk.

CUTTING

Rotary cutter or scissors. Cutting seams ¼ in. wider than ⅝ in. enables seams to be pressed flatter.

INTERFACING

Textured Weft or Hymo Hair Canvas.

THREAD

Silk thread is preferable because it marries with the fabric, rendering almost invisible seams. Good-quality polyester or cotton is also suitable.

NEEDLE

80/12 H.

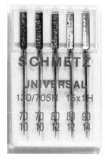

STITCH LENGTH

2.5 mm.

PRESSER FOOT

Standard.

SEAM FINISH

Options if unlined: 1) Pressed open and serged separatly using woolly nylon on the lower looper. 2) Flat fell on lightweights for sporty styles. 3) Hong Kong bound. (See #3 on p. 174, #9 on p. 175, #16 on p. 177.)

PRESSING

Steam iron on wool setting. Press seam as stitched. With seam positioned over a seam roll, seam stick, or half-round to prevent seam allowance show-through on right side, dribble a bead of water in the valley of the seam. Press with steam iron on the wool setting. On right side of fabric, once again, position seam over half-round. Cover with self-fabric press cloth. Press again with steam. Let fabric cool and dry before moving from the pressing surface or fabric will have a puffy appearance. To set crease lines, spray fabric with solution of 3 tablespoons white vinegar to 1 cup water. Cover with a press cloth and iron using plenty of steam and a clapper.

TOPSTITCHING

Options: 1) Use buttonhole twist thread, an N needle, and edge foot or edge-joining foot. Topstitch close to the edge or ¼ in. from the edge. 2) Hand-pick ¼ in. with stitches ¼ in. apart using buttonhole twist or shiny rayon thread. (See #1 and #3 on p. 180, #10 on p. 181.)

CLOSURES

For buttonholes, use a 70/10 HJ needle. Cord buttonholes to prevent stretching. Hand buttonholes are also an option for coats and jackets. (See #1 and #5 on p. 182.)

HEM

Hong Kong finish, enclose raw edges with Seams Great, or serge raw edge. Turn up a 2-in. hem. Press and hand-hem. (See #4 on p. 187.)

Woolens & worsteds

FABRIC FACT

Woolens are softer, fuzzier, have more nap, more stretch and appear spongier than worsteds. Worsteds are harder, smoother, stronger, and more lustrous. They also hold a crease and drape better.

SUITABLE FOR

Fabric weight determines suitable garment. Heavier woolens make great coats. Heavier worsteds make good jackets. Lighter-weight woolens and worsteds can be used for unstructured jackets; draped, shaped, or slightly gathered dresses; wrap skirts; slightly gathered or A-line skirts; or soft tailored pants. Dresses, pants, and skirts must be lined or they will seat out.

SEWING TIPS

Very easy to sew.

Tip: Few home-sewing machines are capable of joining two flat-fell seams at the crotch in heavy fabric. Instead serge one side of the seam allowance, then trim the other. Overlap the serged seam allowance without turning under onto trimmed seam allowance. Topstitch. This forms a fake flat fell that is less bulky and easier to sew. (See #28 on p. 178.)

Wool Gauze

PRESHRINK
Hold steam iron ½ in. above fabric. Dry-clean completed garment when needed.

LAYOUT
"Without nap" layout, double thickness.

MARKING
Tailor's chalk or fabric markers.

CUTTING
Rotary cutter or scissors.

INTERFACING
Silk organza to maintain transparency.

THREAD
Good-quality cotton or polyester.

NEEDLE
70/10H.

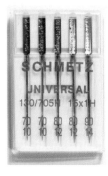

STITCH LENGTH
2.0 mm.

PRESSER FOOT
Standard.

SEAM FINISH
French seams. (See #10 on p. 175.)

PRESSING
Steam iron on wool setting.

TOPSTITCHING
Close to edge, using walking foot to prevent ripples.

CLOSURES
For buttonholes use 70/10 HJ and fine machine embroidery thread to reduce bulk. (See #1 on p. 182.)

HEM
Rolled hem by hand or serged rolled hem. Use differential feed or keep finger behind presser foot to prevent stretching. (See #16 on p. 189.)

Wool gauze

FABRIC FACT
Wool gauze is the least stable fabric in the wool family. It is quite sheer. Since this fabric is weak and filmy, it needs at least 4 in. of ease at bust and hip.

SUITABLE FOR
Loose tops and dresses with slip dress or beautiful slip underneath. Undergarment outline will show.

SEWING TIPS
Do not stretch fabric as you sew. Push into the presser foot.

Tip: Avoid over pressing on wools by using a press cloth made from self-fabric or iron shoe.

Wool Jersey

PRESHRINK

Hold steam iron ½ in. above surface. Dry-clean finished garment. Store garment flat if possible.

LAYOUT

"Without nap" layout, double thickness.

MARKING

Snips in seam allowance, Clo-Chalk, fabric markers.

CUTTING

Rotary cutter or scissors.

INTERFACING

Fuse-Knit or French Fuse.

THREAD

Good-quality silk, cotton, or polyester.

NEEDLE

75 / 11 HS.

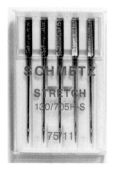

STITCH LENGTH

Tiny zigzag (0.5 mm width, 2.5 mm length).

PRESSER FOOT

Standard.

SEAM FINISH

Options: 1) Sew seams with a small zigzag. This allows the seams to relax as the fabric relaxes. Finish seams with a 3-thread serger. 2) Sew with lightning stitch, then press open. 3) Fake flat-fell seam. (See #12 on p. 175, #21 on p. 177, #27 on p. 178.)

PRESSING

Steam iron on wool setting. On right side use a press cloth or iron shoe to prevent shine. Allow fabric to dry and cool before moving to avoid stretching.

TOPSTITCHING

Close to the edge with the help of edge foot or edge-joining foot or ¼ in. from edge. (See #3 on p. 180, #10 on p. 181.)

CLOSURES

Stabilize buttonhole area with lengthwise-grain interfacing parallel to buttonhole and Solvy above and below fabric. Cord buttonholes in jackets to prevent stretching. Stabilize zipper seam allowances with ½-in. strips of fusible interfacing. Hand-picked zipper is the most attractive. (See #5 on p. 182, #5 on p. 186.)

HEM

Pink or serge raw hem edge. Turn up 1½-in. hem. Topstitch using double-needle ZWI stretch with woolly nylon hand-wrapped on bobbin and Teflon foot. On right side, sew ¼ in. from hem crease. Skip 1 in. and sew another row of double-needle stitching parallel to the first. Loosen top tension until stitches lie flat. (See #18 on p. 176, #24 on p. 190.)

Wool jersey

FABRIC FACT
This is one of those
fabrics that falls into the
"fabric friend" category.
Wool jersey makes up
well in styles where drape
is needed. This fabric
drapes beautifully. Wool
jersey is flattering on the
body, comfortable to
wear, and resists wrinkles.
It is not suitable for skinny pull-on pants because
the fabric is not strong
enough to recover from
prolonged stretch at the
knees and seat.

SUITABLE FOR
Wrap tops, semi-fitted or
full dresses, full pants,
full tops, full or gored
skirts.

SEWING TIPS
Easy to sew.

Tip: Since wool jersey
shrinks both in length
and width it must be
preshrunk. To do this at
home, hold iron ½ in.
above fabric surface,
letting the steam flow
into the fabric. Let
fabric dry completely
before moving. Unless
you have a long table,
this process can be
done easily on the floor.

Wool Melton

PRESHRINK
Hold steam iron ½ in. above fabric surface.

LAYOUT
"With nap" layout—not always necessary but a safe bet. Lay out in single thickness. Use pattern weights because pins tear tissue.

MARKING
Tailor tacks or Clo-Chalk.

CUTTING
Rotary cutter or sharp scissors.

INTERFACING
None—fabric has enough body without it. Stabilize neck and shoulder with stay-tape.

THREAD
Silk thread is the best choice because it marries with the fabric. Good-quality cotton or polyester is also suitable.

NEEDLE
90/14 H.

STITCH LENGTH
3.0 mm to 3.5 mm.

PRESSER FOOT
Teflon.

SEAM FINISH
Butt edges together over 1½-in.-wide wool jersey strip. Machine-sew a featherstitch. This joins the layers of melton while attaching to the strip. Trim down one side of the wool jersey strip, and wrap the other around and hand-stitch. Sew darts in the same manner, cutting out bulk in darts. (See #14 on p. 176.)

PRESSING
Use steam iron on wool setting. Use a piece of wool as press cloth when pressing on the right side.

TOPSTITCHING
Options: 1) Unnecessary when using binding. 2) Hand-pick. (See #1 on p. 180.) 3) Topstitch ⅜ in. from edge using an N needle and topstitching thread, lengthening stitch to 4.0 mm.

CLOSURES
Consider alternate closures: faced buttonhole, button in a seam, button loops, frogs. (See #6, #9, and #10 on p. 183, #12 on p. 184.)

HEM
Eliminate hem allowance. Bind hem edge with wool jersey or faux leather. (See #9 on p. 188.)

Wool melton

FABRIC FACT

Wool melton is a heavily felted, full
wool with a smooth napped surface.
It is very warm to wear but also thick
and bulky if sewn with traditional
sewing methods.

SUITABLE FOR

Keep style simple in coats,
vests, or jackets. Choose a
raglan or dolman sleeve
style. Choose no patterns
with gathers or pleats. In-
seam or welt pockets are
the least bulky. Reduce
bulk whenever desired,
which includes elimi-
nating facings, hems,
and linings. Bind
edges with faux
leather or wool
jersey. Faux
suede binding
is not supple
enough. For a
warm coat that is
not bulky, consider an
unstructured unlined coat
using wool jersey for trim.

SEWING TIPS

If the melton is not too thick,
conventional tailoring methods
can be used. Because melton is bulky,
I like to eliminate the seam allowances and butt edges together.
To use this method of construction,
cut off seam allowances wherever you
plan to use the butt-and-sew method
described under seam finish.

Tip: For barely visible seams in
tailored wool garments, hand-sew
with silk thread.

Seams

Since I have used all of the fabrics in this book to make garments or home-dec projects, I suggest in the text seams and seam finishes that from my experience are the most compatible and attractive for each fabric.

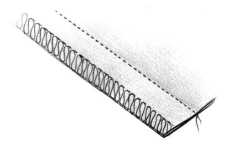

Straight seam, serged together (4)

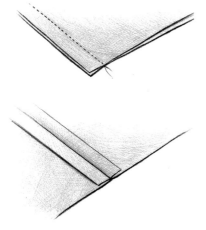

Straight seam, pressed open (1)

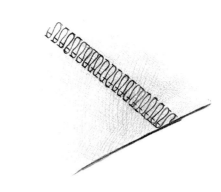

4-thread serged seam (5)

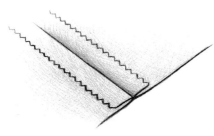

Straight seam, pinked (2)

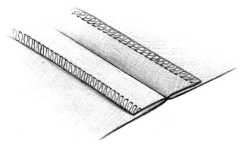

Seam allowances pressed open and serged separately (3)

Triple stitch (6)

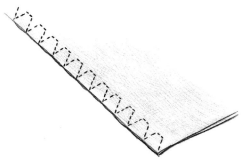

Stretch stitch, fine (7)

Stretch stitch, heavier (8)

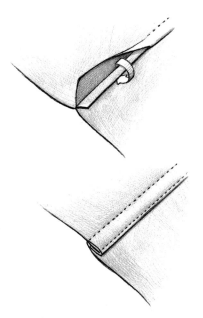

Flat-fell seam (9)

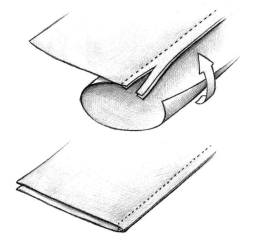

French seam sewn with straight stitch (10)

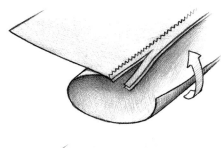

French seam sewn with zigzag stitch (11)

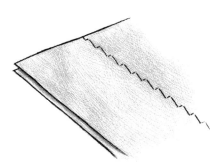

Lightning stitch (12)

Seams

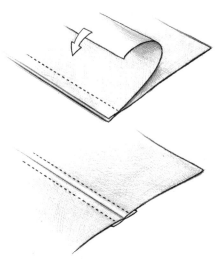

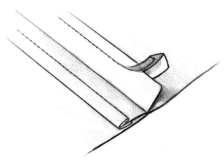

Hong Kong finish on seam allowance (16)

Seam sewn, pressed open, then topstitched down on each side ¼ in. away from seam (13)

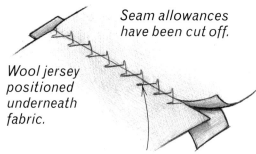

Seam allowances have been cut off.

Wool jersey positioned underneath fabric.

Feather stitch joins seam and wool jersey together.

Butted edges for thick, nonravelling fabrics (14)

Tiny zigzag sewn as seam (17)

½-in. strips of fusible interfacing on seam allowance

Fusible interfacing strips stabilizing seam allowance for zipper (18)

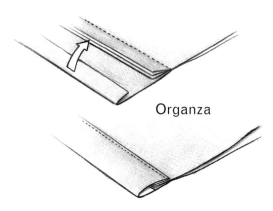

Organza

Seam bound with strip of organza (15)

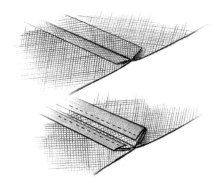

Seam sewn on lace fabric bound on each side of seam with Seams Great (19)

Seams

Seam sewn and bound on each side of the seam allowance with contrasting-color double-fold bias tape (20)

Sew seams wrong sides together, then flatten together toward front. Cover seam allowances with trim or braid and topstitch on both sides of trim.

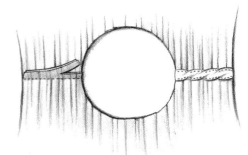

Pleated fabric (24)

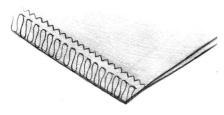

Zigzag stitched and serged (3 thread) (21)

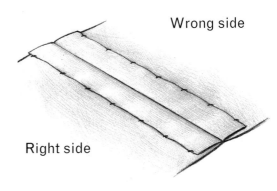

Wrong side

Right side

Seams sewn, pressed open, then hand whipstitched to keep open on each side of seam allowance (25)

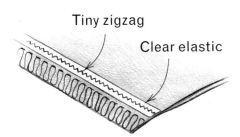

Tiny zigzag

Clear elastic

Zigzag sewn over ¼-in. strip of clear elastic with 4-thread serged line of stitching next to it (22)

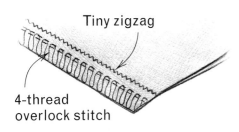

Tiny zigzag

4-thread overlock stitch

4-thread serged seam with tiny zigzag next to it (23)

Lace joined in seam (26)

Seams

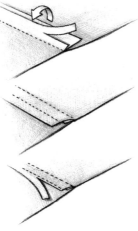

Trim seam allowance then overlap over trimmed seam allowance.

Fake flat-fell seam (27)

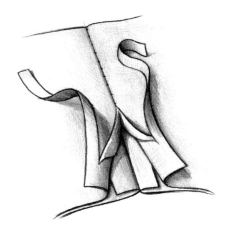

Seam for double-sided wool (30)

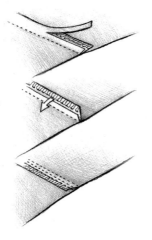

1. Sew seam.

2. Trim one side of seam allowance to ¼ in. Serge the other side along edge at ⅝ in.

3. Overlap serged seam and topstitch over trimmed seam.

Serged fake flat-fell seam (28)

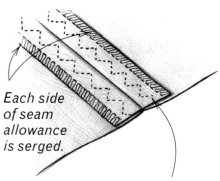

Each side of seam allowance is serged.

Triple-step topstitching on each side to open and flatten seam allowance

Seam on terrycloth (31)

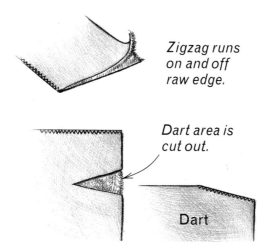

Zigzag runs on and off raw edge.

Dart area is cut out.

Dart

Seam on fur (29)

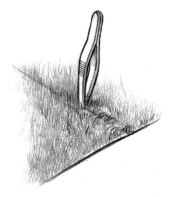

Pick hairs out of seam to right side.

Seam on fur fabric, right side (32)

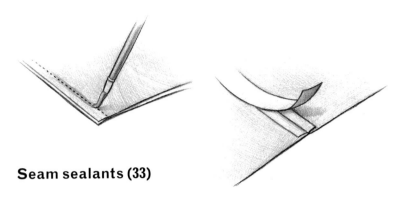

Seam sealants (33)

Sew seam then trim one seam allowance.

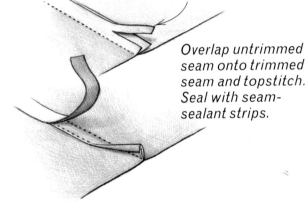

Overlap untrimmed seam onto trimmed seam and topstitch. Seal with seam-sealant strips.

Fake flat fell for sealed seams (34)

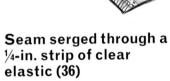

Seam serged through a ¼-in. strip of clear elastic (36)

Flatlock stitch close to edge

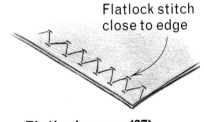

Flatlock seam (37)

Line of glue right next to staystitching within seam allowance

Wear sunglasses or goggles.

Take beads out of seams.

Seam in beaded fabric (35)

Sequin fabric (38)

Details

Certain fabrics lend themselves to machine topstitching, others to serger finishes, and others to hand stitches. Within the text, I suggest treatments that I find the most attractive on a specific fabric. Much of this is personal taste. You, of course, can decide what you like.

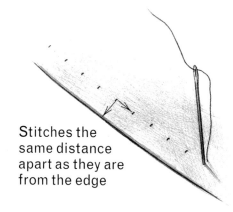

Stitches the same distance apart as they are from the edge

Hand-picking (1)

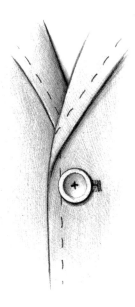

Saddle stitch (4)

Topstitching close to neck edge ⅛ in. from seam (2)

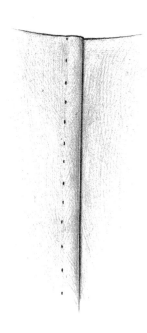

Collar topstitched close to edge (3)

Hand-picked zipper (5)

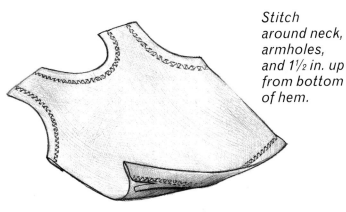

Stitch around neck, armholes, and 1½ in. up from bottom of hem.

Fold the hem to the wrong side and sew it down from the right side. Trim excess fabric close to the seam on the wrong side.

Flatlock stitch (6)

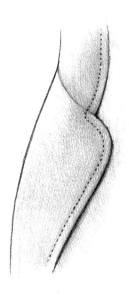

Topstitching on lapel ⅜ in. from edge for hairy fabric like mohair or curly fake fur (9)

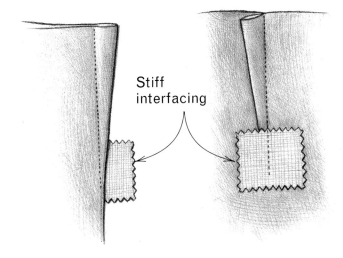

Stiff interfacing

Dart without dimple (7)

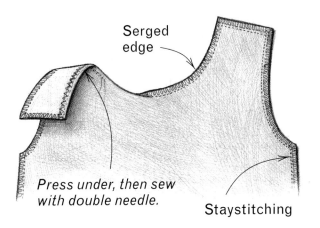

Serged edge

Press under, then sew with double needle.

Staystitching

Topstitching with double needle (8)

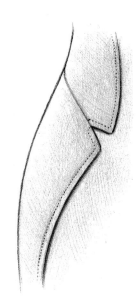

Topstitching on lapel ¼ in. from edge (10)

Closures

Within the text you will find closure suggestions for each fabric. I offer these suggestions based on two things: what is used most often in ready-to-wear and what I have found from my personal experience to be the most compatible.

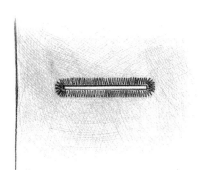

Standard buttonhole for wovens (1)

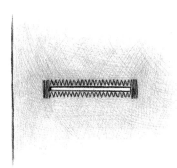

Standard buttonhole for knits (3)

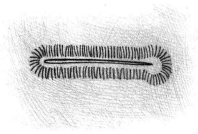

Hand-stitched buttonhole (2)

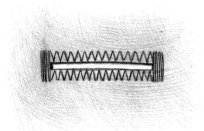

Wider buttonhole with stitches spaced a little wider apart (4)

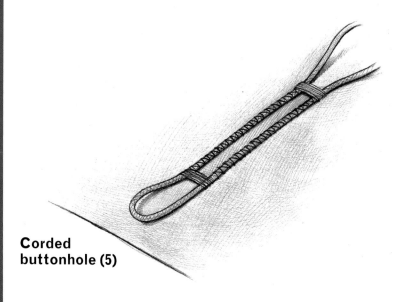

Corded buttonhole (5)

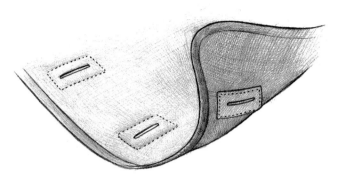

Faced buttonhole (6)

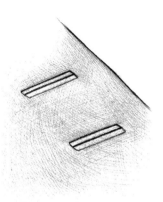

Bound buttonhole (8)

Button loops (9)

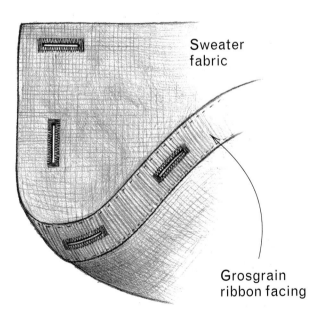

Sweater fabric

Grosgrain ribbon facing

Buttonhole in grosgrain (7)

Buttonhole in seam (10)

Closures

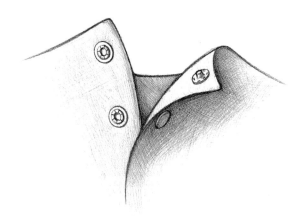

Snaps (11)

Frog closure (12)

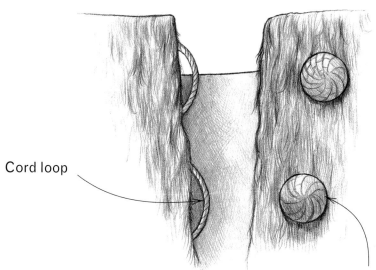

Cord loop

Button loops made in cord with braided buttons (13)

Braided button

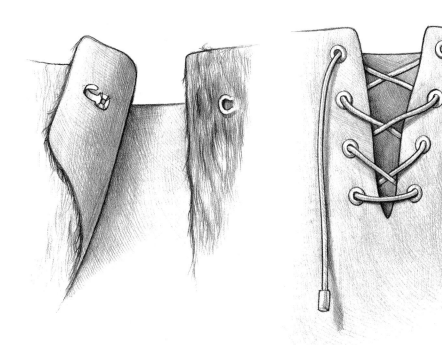

**Oversized fur hooks
on fur fabric (14)**

Eyelets and lacing (15)

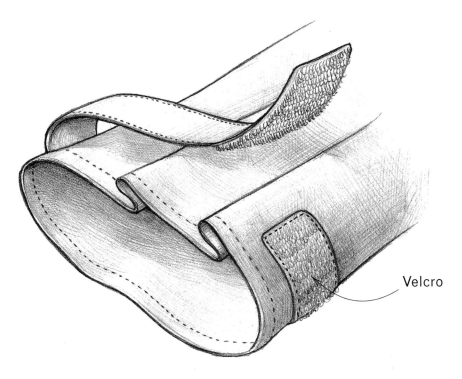

Velcro

Cuff with Velcro strap closure (16)

Closures

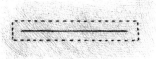

Topstitch ¼-in. rectangle, then cut opening for buttonhole.

Cut-open buttonhole on leather (17)

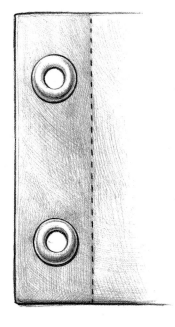

Oversized grommets on canvas (18)

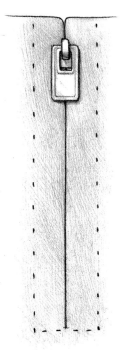

Hand-picked

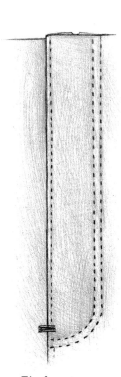

Fly front

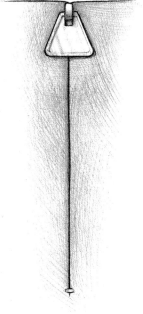

Invisible

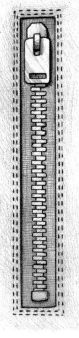

Exposed

Zippers (19)

Within the text you will find hem suggestions, determined by my personal experience with the fabric. My goals were to eliminate bulk, prevent stretching, and render the hem to be either as invisible as possible or an attractive machine detail.

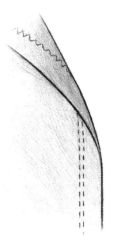

Double-needle hemstitch (1)

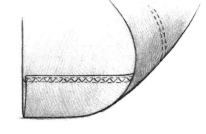

Hand hemstitch (4)

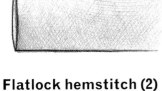

Flatlock hemstitch (2)

Cover hem topstitch (5)

Wrong side

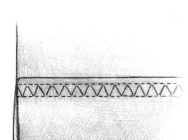

Machine hemstitch (6)

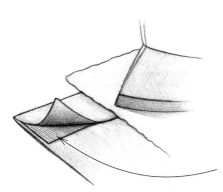

Stitch Witchery

Hem with Stitch Witchery inside (3)

Hems

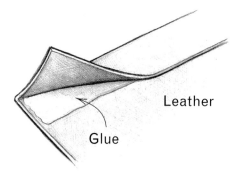

Leather

Glue

Glue within hem (7)

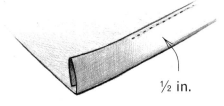

Neckline bound with self-fabric double fold (9)

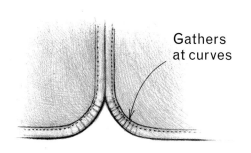

Gathers at curves

Easestitch to gather up curves slightly (8)

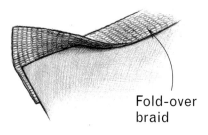

½ in.

Double-fold machine hem (10)

Fold-over braid covering raw edge of fabric (11)

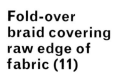

Fold-over braid

Row of decorative stitching

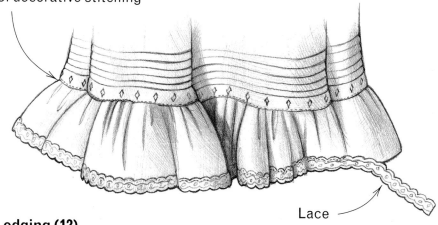

Lace

Lace edging (12)

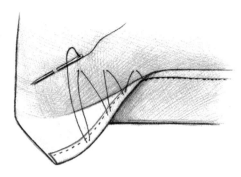

Hong Kong finish on raw edge with hand stitching (13)

With Thread Fuse

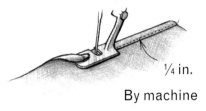

¼ in.

By machine

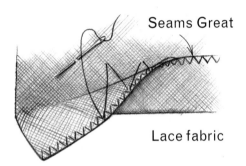

Seams Great

Lace fabric

Seams Great zigzagged on lace fabric (14)

By hand

With serger

Four finishes on a rolled hem (16)

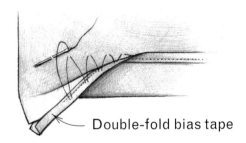

Double-fold bias tape

Raw edge covered with double-fold bias tape (15)

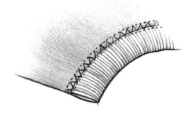

Flatlock with ribbing (17)

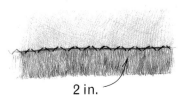

Low-loft fur

High-loft fur (faced with satin bias)

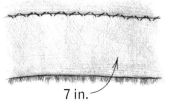

Hems on fur (18)

2 in.

7 in.

Hems

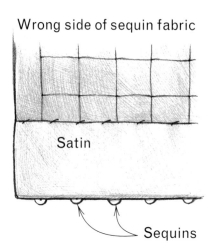

Sequin fabric faced at hem
with 2 in. of smooth satin (19)

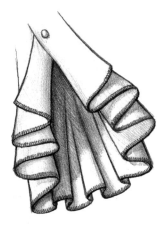

**Ruffles created by serging
over fishing line (20)**

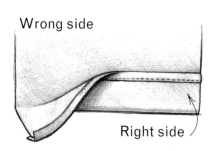

**Raw edge covered with
double-fold bias tape, then
machine stitched (21)**

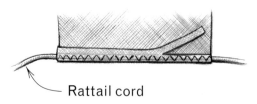

**Zigzag sewn over rattail cord
on bridal net (22)**

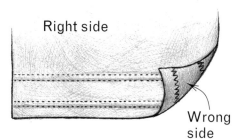

**Two rows of double-needle
stitching 1 in. apart (23)**

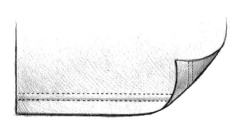

**Double row of topstitching not
done with double needle (24)**

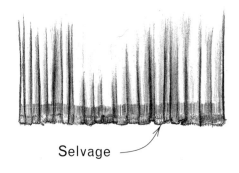

**Pleated fabric with selvage
as hem (25)**

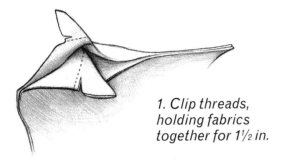

1. Clip threads, holding fabrics together for 1½ in.

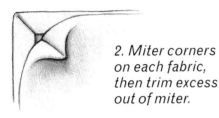

2. Miter corners on each fabric, then trim excess out of miter.

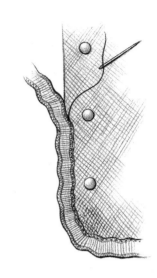

Lace trim on lace (28)

3. Turn right side out and press.

4. Hand-stitch corners together invisibly. Fold in, then hand tack.

Hem for double-faced wool (26)

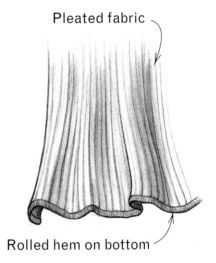

Pleated fabric

Rolled hem on bottom

Lettuce leaf hem serged (29)

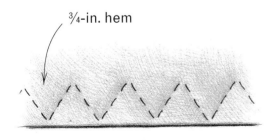

¾-in. hem

Triple-step zigzag (27)

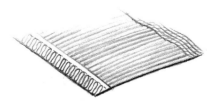

Ribbing with 4-thread serger over ¼-in. strip of elastic (30)

Hems

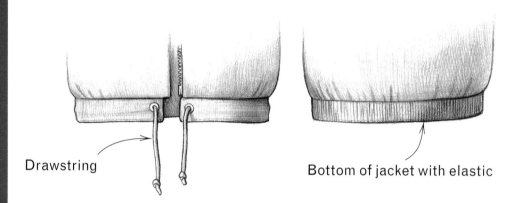

Drawstring

Bottom of jacket with elastic

Casings on jacket with elastic (31)

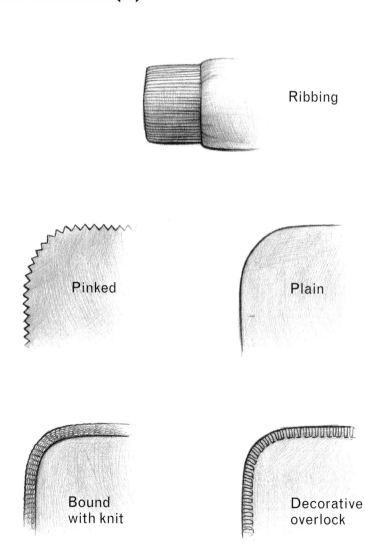

Ribbing

Pinked

Plain

Bound
with knit

Decorative
overlock

**Hem finishes
for fleece (32)**

Glossary

ACCORDIAN-PLEATED FABRIC
Narrow ⅛-in. to ½-in. pleats that resemble folds in an accordion. (Sew as pre-pleated fabrics; see p. 80.)

ACETATE
A filament fiber made from acetate with a crisp hand and high luster. Drapes well. Acetate woven fabric is often used for linings, but it shows perspiration stains. (Sew as silk crepe de chine; see p. 100.)

ACRYLIC
A synthetic fiber that has a soft hand and good wrinkle resistance. It can be machine-washed and machine-dried, but it tends to pill easily. It is often used in blankets and socks. (Sew as wool flannel; see p. 166.)

ADMIRALTY CLOTH
Melton cloth often used in military uniforms and pea coats. (Sew as wool melton; see p. 172.)

AEROZIP POLYESTER
Used for insulation in outerwear. (Sew as insulation; see p. 52.)

AIDA CANVAS
Stiff, coarse fabric used for needlework. (Sew as canvas; see p. 16.)

ALBERT CLOTH
A reversible wool double cloth with different colors on front and back. Used for coats. (Sew as wool double cloth; see p. 164.)

ALENÇON LACE
A needlepoint lace with fine net background with cord outlining design. (Sew as lace; see p. 60.)

ALPACA, SOFT
Lustrous, very-warm-to-wear fabric made from Llama fleece. Used for coats and shawls. (Sew as cashmere; see p. 18.)

AMBIANCE
A lightweight silk-like rayon lining manufactured by Bemberg. Hand-washable. (Sew as China silk; see p. 22.)

ANGORA
The hair of the angora goat, not the angora rabbit, which produces mohair. (Sew as mohair; see p. 76.)

BATIK
Any fabric created by resist-dyeing using wax as a resist. After the wax is removed, fabric is colored where dye has gone through wax cracks. Fabric is often used for shirts, skirts, and loose dresses. (Sew as cotton shirting; see p. 32.)

BEMBERG
A trademark of Bemberg SPA, Italy, this rayon lining material has a soft, silk-like quality and is available in several weights. Available from American Bemberg Corp. (Sew lightweight Bemberg as China silk; see p. 22. Sew heavy-weight Bemberg as silk noil; see p. 108.)

BENGALINE
A lustrous, durable, warp-faced fabric with corded appearance most often used in millinery, ribbons, and suits. (Sew as gabardine; see p. 46.)

BOTANY WOOL
Originally referred to Australian wool of fine quality but now refers to fine wool from all over the world. (Sew as wool worsted; see p. 166.)

BOYNGE
Thermal underwear fabric. (Sew as lightweight knit; see p. 54.)

BROADCLOTH
A fine, closely woven, lustrous cotton or poly-cotton blend with an unbalanced weave that creates a fine rib. An excellent shirting material because of its soft but firm finish. (Sew as cotton shirting; see p. 32.)

BROCADE
A heavy jacquard woven fabric with raised floral or geometric patterns that emphasize surface contrast or color. (Sew as upholstery; see p. 138.)

BUCKRAM
A coarse, stiff, plain open-weave fabric used as a stiffener. (Sew as canvas; see p. 16.)

BURLAP
A coarse, plain-weave fabric sometimes used for curtains. Fades in direct sun. (Sew as canvas; see p. 16.)

BURN-OUT FABRIC
Made from two different yarns where pattern is created by burning out one yarn with a chemical. (Cut as velvet; see p. 142. Sew as chiffon; see p. 98.)

CABRETTA
A fine lightweight goatskin. Excellent choice for garment sewing, especially pants. (Sew as leather; see p. 64.)

CALICO
A plain cotton weave with a typically busy, small floral pattern. (Sew as cotton shirting; see p. 32.)

CAMBRIC
A soft plain-weave cloth or linen with a slight luster used for handkerchiefs, aprons, and underwear. (Sew as cotton batiste; see p. 26.)

Glossary

CAVALRY TWILL
A popular fabric for military uniforms. Its distinct twill weave makes it an excellent choice for a jacket or coat. Fabric is very wrinkle resistant. (Sew as wool flannel; see p. 166.)

CHAMBRAY
Has the appearance of very fine denim, with a plain weave using colored warp and white weft. Makes great shirts and pajamas. (Sew as cotton shirting; see p. 32.)

CHAMOIS
Lightweight leather from sheepskin. Used for buffing cars and American Indian–inspired garments. (Sew as suede; see p. 124.)

CHARMELAINE
A wool twill dress fabric with a ribbed face and smooth back. (Sew as wool gabardine; see p. 46.)

CHINA SILK
A lightweight, plain woven silk suitable for lining garments because it breathes and doesn't add bulk. It wrinkles, is not very durable, and should not be used as fashion fabric. (See p. 22.)

CHINTZ
Plain-weave cotton fabric with a glazed finish often used for slipcovers and curtains. (Sew as cotton piqué; see p. 30.)

CHINO
A durable twill-cotton fabric with a slight sheen that makes excellent work clothes or casual pants. (Sew as cotton piqué; see p. 30.)

COOL WOOL
A trade name used to denote a lightweight "tropical" wool. Armani suits are often made in this fabric. (Sew as wool crepe; see p. 162.)

COVERT
A durable twill-weave fabric made from tightly twisted yarns. Wool covert makes an excellent top coat that can be waterproofed. Cotton covert makes good work clothes or sportswear. (Sew as wool gabardine; see p. 46.)

CREPE-BACKED SATIN
A reversible satin weave with one side dull and crepe-looking, the other shiny and smooth. Because of its wide color range and affordability, crepe-backed satin is often used in bridesmaids' dresses and is flattering when cut on the bias. Opposite sides used together create very interesting design elements. (Sew as satin; see p. 90.)

CRINKLED
Puckered or wrinkled effects created in the fabric construction or in the finishing. Great fabrics for creating texture in an ensemble. (Sew as crinkle cotton; see p. 36.)

CRUSHED VELVET
Velvet that's been processed to have an irregular surface. (Sew as velvet; see p. 142.)

CUT VELVET
Patterned velvet figures on sheer background fabric of chiffon, georgette, or voile. (Cut as velvet; see p. 142. Sew as chiffon; see p. 98.)

DACRON
A trademark of Du Pont, this polyester is an old favorite for house dresses. (Sew as polyester silky but cut on lengthwise grain; see p. 78.)

DEERSKIN
Soft, supple leather skin from deer hide. Makes first-quality garments, especially soft shirts, loose pants,

and skirts. (Sew as leather; see p. 64.)

DONEGAL TWEEDS
A rather coarse, wrinkle-resistant multicolored wool most often used in men's sports jackets. (Sew as wool worsted; see p. 166.)

DOTTED SWISS
A sheer cotton or nylon fabric patterned with small dots that are woven in or glued on. Makes good summer blouses and curtains. (Sew as cotton batiste; see p. 26.)

DRILL
A strong, dense, medium- to heavy-weight cotton of twill weave. Used for uniforms, lining shoes, work clothes, and mattress ticking. (Sew as denim; see p. 38.)

DUCHESSE SATIN
A highly lustrous, smooth, very finely woven silk fabric. Used in bridal or evening wear where volume without bulk is desired. (Sew as satin; see p. 90.)

DUCK
A durable, plain-weave cotton that is flexible. Used for sails, tents, and awnings. (Sew as canvas; see p. 16.)

EGYPTIAN COTTON
A high-quality long staple cotton used in the finest sheets. (Sew as cotton shirting; see p. 32.)

ENGLISH NET
A cotton netting with a hexagonal weave that dyes well. Used in evening wear for sheer sections and as underlining in bodices. (Sew as tulle and net; see p. 136.)

EYELET
Cutouts with stitching outlining them on a base fabric of batiste, lawn,

broadcloth, organdy, or pique used in summer blouses and children's dresses. (Sew according to base fabric.)

FACILE
A trademark of Skinner Co., this faux suede is lightweight and drapes better than Ultrasuede. (Sew as faux suede; see p. 44.)

FAILLE
A flat ribbed fabric with a light luster. Fabric has body but drapes and tailors well. Comes in a wide variety of colors. Makes beautiful spring suits and coats. (Sew as satin; see p. 90.)

FELT
A non-woven, matted material made from man-made fibers used in table covers and crafts. Hat felt contains animal fur. Wool felt is used as interfacing under highly embellished garment details to support weight. (Sew as wool melton; see p. 172.)

FLAX
Used to make linen. (Sew as linen; see p. 66.)

FUJI SILK
A lightweight, plain-weave silk used in blouses. (Sew as silk shantung; see p. 114.)

FUKUSA
A silk square used in Japan to wrap gifts. Can be combined in garments for beautiful effects. (Sew as rayon crepe; see p. 86.)

GAUZE
A fine, transparent, plain-weave fabric with open texture. (Sew as unstable knit; see p. 58.)

GINGHAM
A lightweight plain-weave fabric often woven in checks. Great for pattern pretests. (Sew as cotton shirting; see p. 32.)

GORE-TEX
A trademark of WL Gore and Assoc. Inc., this porous fabric repels water but allows body moisture to escape, making it comfortable for active outerwear. (Sew as waterproof breathables; see p. 152.)

GROSGRAIN
A closely woven ribbed ribbon made with a rayon warp. Must be preshrunk.

HABUTAI
A soft, lightweight plain-weave silk usually referred to as China silk. (Sew as China silk; see p. 22.)

HANDKERCHIEF LINEN
A plain weave of the lightest weight linen. Used for handkerchiefs, blouses, and bias binding. (Sew as cotton batiste; see p. 26.)

HARRIS TWEED
A woolen fabric hand-woven on the islands off the coast of Scotland. It is wrinkle resistant and often used in men's sport jackets. (Sew as wool worsted; see p. 166.)

HOPSACKING
A coarse, loosely woven fabric woven in hopsack or basket weave. Burlap is a very rough hopsack example. Cotton or linen hopsacking is more pliable and can be used in lightweight, loose coats. (Sew as linen; see p. 66.)

JACONET
A fine, sheer plain-weave cotton fabric used in children's summer clothing. (Sew as cotton batiste; see p. 26.)

JACQUARD
A weaving system that can produce woven designs of a large size.

LAWN
A finely woven, semi-crisp fabric woven in cotton or linen. It is primarily used in heirloom dresses, blouses, collars, and cuffs. Also makes great underlining. (Sew as cotton batiste; see p. 26.)

LEATHERETTE
A coated fabric that simulates leather. Used in upholstery. (Sew as vinyl; see p. 146.)

LIBERTY
A trademark of Liberty Ltd. England for hand-blocked floral prints in silk, rayon, cotton, and wool challis.

LODEN CLOTH
A thick, soft, oily green wool fabric that repels water and is typically seen in coatings. (Sew as wool melton; see p. 172.)

MADRAS
A fine cotton, hand loomed in the Madras region of India dyed with natural dyes. (Sew as cotton shirting; see p. 32.)

MATELASSE
A fabric with crepe and ordinary yarn interfaced in the warp. When the crepe yarn shrinks, it causes the ordinary yarn to pucker, creating raised patterns. Can be made in cotton, silk, or wool. (Sew as pleated fabric; see p. 80.)

MERINO WOOL
A very fine, dense wool from the merino sheep. Takes dye well. (Sew as wool flannel; see p. 166.)

Glossary

MESH
Woven, knitted, crocheted, lace, or knotted with open spaces between yarns. Fabric is supple and elastic. Used in men's sport shirts. Very lightweight mesh is used in evening wear. (Sew as tulle and net; see p. 136.)

MOHAIR
A durable and resilient long-hair fabric made from the angora goat. (See p. 76.)

MOIRÉ
A wavy, water-like pattern produced onto a fabric surface by engraved rollers during the finishing process.

MOLESKIN
A heavy, strong cotton woven with coarse yarns used in work clothes. (Sew as denim; see p. 38.)

MOMME
A Japanese unit of weight for silk fabrics.

MONK'S CLOTH
A heavy coarse cotton fabric with a loose basket weave. Used in draperies, slipcovers, and upholstery. (Sew as canvas; see p. 16.)

MUSLIN
A firm plain-weave cotton found in many weights. Great for pattern pretests. (Sew as cotton shirting; see p. 32.)

NAPA
A soft, thin, very drapey leather skin used for quality garments. (Sew as leather; see p. 64.)

OILCLOTH
(1) An oil-coated fabric with a waterproof surface. Clean with water. Used for table or shelf covers. (Sew as vinyl; see p. 146.) (2) A lightweight silk that has been lightly coated with oil, making the fabric waterproof. (Sew as sandwashed silk; see p. 112.)

ORGANDY
A very fine, sheer cotton with a crisp hand. (Sew as organza; see p. 110.)

OTTOMAN
A firm, lustrous fabric with rounded horizontal cord lines that give the fabric texture. Terrific for collar and cuff contrasts. (Sew as brocade; see p. 94.)

OXFORD CLOTH
A plain weave with twice as many threads in the warp as in the weft, resulting in a basketweave. (Sew as cotton shirting; see p. 32.)

PANNÉ SATIN
A high-gloss satin fabric. (Sew as satin; see p. 90.)

PANNÉ VELVET
Often with a knitted base, pile on this velvet is pressed down in one direction, resulting in a shiny appearance. (Cut as velvet; see p. 142. Sew as stable knit; see p. 54.)

PATENT LEATHER
Shiny, hard, smooth leather created by applying a solution that hardens to the surface of the leather. (Sew as vinyl but use a leather NTW needle; see p. 146.)

PEAU DE SOIE
A heavy soft silk with a satin finish. (Sew as satin; see p. 90.)

PERCALE
A lightweight firm cotton with a balanced weave that can be piece-dyed or printed. (Sew as cotton shirting; see p. 32.)

PETERSHAM
A flexible, moldable ribbed rayon/cotton ribbon used in hat bands or as waistline facings. Must be preshrunk. (Sew as cotton piqué; see p. 30.)

PIGSKIN
A sueded leather skin that can be drapey or firm depending on the dye lot. Works well in jackets, slim pants, and straight skirts. Usually does not drape well enough for fuller-style garments. (Sew as suede; see p. 124.)

PIMA COTTON
A very fine American Egyptian cotton that is great for underlining. (Sew as cotton batiste; see p. 26.)

PLISSE
A puckered or crinkled cotton. (Sew as crinkle cotton; see p. 36.)

POINT D'ESPRIT
A netting with a rectangular dot in a regular, allover pattern. (Sew as tulle and net; see p. 136.)

PONGEE
A plain-weave, medium-weight silk with a finer warp than weft that feels like a starched China silk. Suitable for tailored blouses. (Sew as silk tussah; see p. 118.)

POPLIN
Fabric with a similar weave to broadcloth but the rib is larger and the fabric heavier. (Sew as cotton damask; see p. 28.)

POWERNET
A four-way stretch fabric often used for girdles. (Sew as stable knit; see p. 54.)

QUIANA
This trade name for a nylon fiber was originated by Du Pont. Although this fiber is no longer available due

to problems with heat resistance, it was made up into many different weaves. (Sew as satin; see p. 90.)

RASCHEL KNIT
A warp-knitted fabric that comes in a variety of patterns. (Sew as stable knits; see p. 54.)

SANDWASHED
Fabric on which sand or other abrasives have been used to give a worn or faded appearance with a soft hand. (Sew as sandwashed silk; see p. 112.)

SATEEN
Fabric made of long staple cotton or filament yarns to produce a strong, lustrous surface. (Sew as cotton damask; see p. 28.)

SEA ISLAND COTTON
The finest grade of cotton. (Sew as cotton batiste; see p. 26.)

SEERSUCKER
A permanently crinkled cotton stripe. Crinkle is produced in the weave and is not destroyed by heat. (See p. 36.)

SHARKSKIN
A worsted wool with a mottled effect often found in men's suitings. A lighter weight in cotton is used in sportswear and uniforms. (Sew as worsted wool; see p. 166.)

SHEARLING
A leather made from pelts that have a short, pulled wool surface. (Sew as faux fur but use a leather NTW needle; see p. 40.)

SHEEPSKIN
Suede produced from a special breed of sheep that grows hair rather than wool. (Sew as faux fur but use a leather NTW needle; see p. 40.)

SILK BROADCLOTH
A fine, closely woven silk with a fine rib. (Sew as sandwashed silk; see p. 112.)

SPANDEX
A manufactured fiber of at least 85% polyurethane with excellent recovery and flexibility. (Sew as Lycra; see p. 72.)

SURAH
A soft, lightweight lustrous silk characterized by fine twill lines. Because it isn't durable, it's best used in ties and vest fronts. (Sew as silk crepe de chine; see p. 100.)

SWISS COTTON
A fine, sheer, crisp cotton. (Sew as cotton shirting; see p. 32.)

THERMOLITE
A Du Pont-trademarked fabric made from inter-locked polyester that is coated to be slippery and durable. (Sew as water and wind resistant; see p. 150.)

THERMOLOFT
A Du Pont-trademarked insulation fabric. (Sew as insulation; see p. 52.)

THINSULATE
A thermal insulation that can't be dry cleaned. It provides twice the insulation of similar thicknesses of polyester, down, or wool. (Sew as insulation; see p. 52.)

TICKING
A durable plain, twill- or satin-weave cotton fabric most often used as covering for mattresses and pillows and sometimes for upholstery. (Sew as denim; see p. 38.)

TRIACETATE
A modified acetate fiber that is stronger than acetate when wet, with greater resistance to heat, shrinking, wrinkling, and fading. (See p. 152.)

TRICOT
A warp knit fabric with a horizontal rib used often in women's lingerie. Makes a great lining for knitted pants. Fusible tricot makes an excellent lightweight interfacing. (Sew as unstable knits; see p. 58.)

TROPICAL WORSTEDS
Lightweight suiting made of highly twisted yarns that permit air circulation. One yard weighs 7½ ounces to 10 ounces. (Sew as worsted wool; see p. 166.)

VELOUR
A woven or knitted pile fabric that lies in one direction. (Sew as velvet; see p. 142.)

VICUNA
The finest wool woven from a small South American relative of the camel. Very soft to touch and very warm to wear. (Sew as cashmere; see p. 18.)

VISCOSE
A term often used inter-changeably with rayon. (Sew as rayon challis; see p. 84.)

WHIPCORD
A strong worsted natural or manufactured fabric with an upright twill weave. Very resistant to wrinkling or stretching out of shape. This fabric is coarser and a heavier texture than gabardine and is used in riding habits, uniforms, sportswear, and coatings. (Sew as denim; see p. 38.)

Sources

ACTIVE TRIMMING COMPANY
250 W. 39th St.
New York, NY 10018
(800) 878-6336, (212) 921-7114
Brass and aluminum zippers and large selection of decorative pulls. Free catalog.

ART MAX FABRICS
250 W. 40th St.
New York, NY 10018
(212) 398-0755
Pleated fabric 45 in. wide.

BAER FABRICS
515 E. Market St.
Louisville, KY 40202
(502) 583-5521
Very large store with fine fabrics, costume fabrics, and oodles of buttons.

CAROL'S ZOO
Carol Cruise
992 Coral Ridge Circle
Rodeo, CA 94572
(510) 245-2020
Huge selection of unusual faux fur as well as the best stuffed animal patterns available.

CLOTILDE
B3000
Louisiana, MO 63353-3000
(800) 772-2891
www.clotilde.com
Mail-order notions.

CY RUDNICK FABRICS
2450 Grand Ave.
Kansas City, MO 64108
(816) 842-7808
Fine dress fabrics as well as Esther's Pullover Pattern.

FABRICS FOR THE GREAT OUTDOORS
60 Bristol Rd. E. #9
Mississauga, ON L4Z 3K8
Canada
(800) 798-5885, (905) 712-4254
www.fabrics-outdoors.ca
Huge selection of outerwear fabrics and patterns. Very knowledgeable staff that is happy to answer questions about fabric to suit your needs. Free catalog.

FABULOUS FURS
20 W. Pike St.
Covington, KY 41011
(800) 848-4650, (606) 291-3300
www.FabulousFurs.com
Faux leathers and furs.

FROSTLINE KITS
2325 River Rd.
Grand Junction, CO
    81505-2525
(800) 548-7872
www.frostlinekits.com
Precut kits for outdoor clothing and sleeping bags.

GREENBERG & HAMMER, INC.
24 W. 57th St.
New York, NY 10019-3918
(800) 955-5135, (212) 246-2835
Interfacing and insulation fabrics as well as tailoring supplies.

HABERMAN'S FABRICS
117 W. Fourth St.
Royal Oak, MI 48067
(248) 541-0010
Great selection of Lycra-blend fabrics as well as other fine fabrics.

KAREN'S KREATIONS
Karen Rudman
6542 125th Ave. SE
Bellevue, WA 98006
(425) 643-9809
Good mail-order source for boiled wool.

MARYANNE'S FABRICS, ETC.
3965 Phelan #106
Beaumont, TX 77707
(409) 838-3965
Well-chosen fine fabrics.

MATERIAL MAP
95 Fifth Ave.
San Francisco, CA 94118
(415) 386-0440
www.sandrabetzina.com
Compiled by Sandra Betzina and Linda Jones. Shows more than 300 stores across the country, what they specialize in, and how to get to them. $14.95 PPD.

MENDEL'S FAR OUT FABRICS
1556 Haight St.
San Francisco, CA 94117
(415) 621-1287
www.mendels.com
Huge selection of ethnic and costume fabrics.

NANCY'S NOTIONS
PO Box 683
Beaver Dam, WI 53916-0683
(800) 833-0690, (920) 887-0391
www.nancysnotions.com
Mail-order notions.

POWER SEWING
95 Fifth Ave.
San Francisco, CA 94118
(415) 386-0440
www.sandrabetzina.com
Books and videos on a variety of sewing subjects including fitting, construction, and lining garments. Free brochure.

SAN FRANCISCO PLEATING COMPANY
425 Second St., 5th Floor
San Francisco, CA 94107
(415) 982-3003

THE SEWING PLACE
18476 Prospect Rd.
Saratoga, CA 95070
(800) 587-3937, (408) 252-8444
www.thesewingplace.com
Huge selection of mail-order slinky knit.

SPIEGELHOFF'S STRETCH & SEW FABRICS
4901 Washington Ave.
Racine, WI 53408
(414) 632-2660
Good selection of knits and mail-order polarfleece.

STONEMOUNTAIN & DAUGHTER
2518 Shattuck Ave.
Berkeley, CA 94704
(510) 845-6106
Ethnic and fashion fabric.

TANDY LEATHER
(800) 555-3130
www.tandyleather.com
Leather and leather craft supplies.

THAI SILKS

252 State St.
Los Altos, CA 94022
(800) 722-SILK, (650) 948-8611
www.thaisilks.com
Mail-order business for all types of silks.

THINGS JAPANESE

9805 N.E. 116th St., Suite 7160
Kirkland, WA 98034
(425) 821-2287
Huge selection of silk threads and silk dyes.

THRIFTY NEEDLE

3233 Amber St.
Philadelphia, PA 19134
(800) 324-9927
Mail-order sweater bodies.

TWILL AND TUCK

Linda Curtis
106 N. Washington St.
Ritzville, WA 99169
(509) 659-1913
Incredible hand-woven fabrics and book on sewing with hand-wovens called Sew Something Special.

VOGUE FABRICS

618 Hartrey Ave.
Evanston, IL 60202
(800) 433-4313, (708) 864-9600
Huge selection of mail-order fashion fabrics

ALTERNATIVE PATTERN COMPANIES

BIRCH STREET CLOTHING

PO Box 6901
San Mateo, CA 94403
(415) 578-9729
www.birchstreetclothing.com
Patterns and snaps (patterns have ¼-in. seam allowances and snaps).

DESIGN AND SEW

Lois Ericson
PO Box 5222
Salem, OR 97304
(503) 364-6285
www.DesignandSew.com

D'LEAS PATTERNS

2719 E. Third Ave.
Denver, CO 80206
(303) 388-5665

DOS DE TEJAS

Karen Odam
PO Box 1636
Sherman, TX 75091
(800) 883-5278, (903) 893-0064
www.DosdeTejas.com

ENCORE DESIGNS

Debbie Walkowski
2527 225th Pl. NE
Redmond, WA 98053
(425) 895-3077

GHEE'S

2620 Centenary #2-250
Shreveport, LA 71104
(318) 226-1701
www.ghees.com

GREAT COPY PATTERNS

Spiegelhoff's Stretch & Sew Fabrics
Ruthann Spiegelhoff
4901 Washington Ave.
Racine, WI 53408
(414) 632-2660

HARRIET BASKETT

1608 Maycraft Rd.
Virginia Beach, VA 23455
(804) 460-2395

JUDY BISHOP DESIGNS

24603 Island Ave.
Carson, CA 90745
(310) 835-6022

KWIK SEW

3000 Washington Ave. N.
Minneapolis, MN 55411-1699
(888) 594-5739, (612) 521-7651
www.kwiksew.com

LA FRED

4200 Park Blvd., Suite 102
Oakland, CA 94602
www.getcreativeshow.com/lafred.htm

LJ DESIGNS

Lyla Messinger
PO Box 21116
Reno, NV 89515-1116
(702) 853-2207
www.sewnet.com/ljdesigns

PARK BENCH PATTERNS

Mary Lou Rankin
PO Box 1089
Petaluma, CA 94953-1089
(707) 781-9142
www.sewnet.com/parkbench

PATTERNS FOR EVERY BODY

Gale Hazen
The Sewing Place
18476 Prospect Rd.
Saratoga, CA 95070
(408) 252-8444
www.thesewingplace.com

REVISIONS

Diane Ericson
PO Box 7404
Carmel, CA 93921
(408) 659-1989
www.ReVisions-Ericson.com

SEW BABY

313 Mattis #116
Champaign, IL 61821
(800) 249-1907
www.sewbaby.com

SEWING WORKSHOP

2010 Balboa
San Francisco, CA 94121
(800) 466-1599
www.sewingworkshop.com

SILHOUETTES

Peggy Sagers
305 Spring Creek Village #326
Dallas, TX 75248
(972) 960-7373

STRETCH & SEW

PO Box 25306
Tempe, AZ 85285
(800) 547-7717, (602) 966-1462
www.stretch-and-sew.com

SUNDROP TEXTILES

140-1140 Austin Ave.
Coquitiam, BC V3K 3P5
Canada
(604) 936-5236

Index

Note: References in italic indicate an illustration. References in bold indicate a glossary entry.

Index

Threads Books

Look for these and other Taunton Press titles at your local bookstore. You can order them direct by calling (800) 888-8286 or by visiting our website at www.taunton.com. Call for a free catalog.

- Scarves to Make
- Fine Embellishment Techniques
- Just Pockets
- Sew the New Fleece
- The Sewing Machine Guide
- Fine Machine Sewing
- 50 Heirloom Buttons to Make
- Couture Sewing Techniques
- Shirtmaking
- Beyond the Pattern
- Distinctive Details
- Fit and Fabric
- Fitting Solutions
- Fitting Your Figure
- Great Quilting Techniques
- Great Sewn Clothes
- Jackets, Coats and Suits
- Quilts and Quilting
- Sewing Tips & Trade Secrets
- Stitchery and Needle Lace
- Techniques for Casual Clothes
- Ribbon Knits
- The Jean Moss Book of World Knits
- The Knit Hat Book
- Knitted Sweater Style
- Knitting Tips and Trade Secrets
- Hand-Manipulated Stitches for
    Machine Knitters
- Alice Starmore's Book of Fair Isle
    Knitting
- Great Knits
- Hand-Knitting Techniques
- Knitting Around the World
- Colorful Knitwear Design
- American Country Needlepoint

Sewing Companion Library:
- Easy Guide to Serging Fine Fabrics
- Easy Guide to Sewing Blouses
- Easy Guide to Sewing Jackets
- Easy Guide to Sewing Linings
- Easy Guide to Sewing Pants
- Easy Guide to Sewing Skirts